Get Sales Focused

Rethinking and Revolutionising Sales Forces and Sales Results

Adele Crane

A LEADING AUSTRALIAN SALES DEVELOPER

Second Edition

National Library of Australia Cataloguing-in-publication data:

Get Sales Focused:
Rethinking and Revolutionising Sales Forces and Sales Results
ISBN: 0-646-41490-9
ISBN 13: 9780646414904

Distributed by: BookSurge, LLC, an Amazon.com Company
Cover Design by Adcore Creative, Australia

Other Books and Publications by the Author:
Get Sales Focused: Third Edition 2010
Building the Most Effective Sales Force in the World: the era post the
global financial crisis

Mastering Sales™ - *www.masteringsales.com*

The New York Times

"An endless number of books have been written on mastering sales techniques and improving a company's bottom line. While many of them contain helpful tips and ideas, few of them delve beyond the how-to's of managing the sales process, and fewer still venture into the inner workings of corporate culture, where the secrets of success—and often failure—lie.

In *Get Sales Focused: Rethinking and Revolutionising Sales Forces and Sales Results*, experienced author, consultant and sales developer Adele Crane sets the bar high for improving sales, embracing change and mastering the business skills necessary for success in the 21st century. An ambitious work that fully delivers on its promise, Crane's essential book provides business owners, managers and sales professionals all of the tools needed to become industry leaders in this rapidly changing world.

The author's proven methods begin with an examination of the cultural shifts in business and the evolution of sales managers over time. How to identify your own company's culture—an often painful and confrontational practice—is vital for developing a successful culture focused on sales, as well as avoiding complacency and coping with change, factors that can doom even the most well-meaning and experienced business professionals. In addition, *Get Sales Focused: Rethinking and Revolutionising Sales Forces and Sales Results* is packed with proven techniques that include trends, research and case studies so that you can put these specific ideas to work for you.

Rather than resorting to rhetorical tricks and tired adages, Crane's well-written and highly effective book walks you through the steps necessary to actually make those hard but necessary changes in yourself and your organization, which sets this book apart as a must-have guide for implementation. Infused with business smarts, a sense of humour and all the strategies you need to take your team to the next level.

Get Sales Focused: Rethinking and Revolutionising Sales Forces and Sales Results delivers a clear and patently actionable message to assist you achieve your goals.

There's no need to ever read another book on this subject."

Contents

About the Author

Adele Crane is a leading and highly respected international business consultant with over twenty-five years experience working in Australia, New Zealand, North America, United Kingdom, and South Africa. Adele's consultancy work has produce results for literally hundreds of organisations through many different industries through change management programmes and improving sales force effectiveness. She is arguably one of the foremost authorities on sales forces in the world today. Her success has received recognition in major media forums across the world. Her expertise in leading change and growth is widely relied upon. Adele commissions research to ensure the information provided to clients is current and will give them a competitive advantage.

As a consultant, Adele works with a limited number of highly motivated clients across the world who are striving to achieve world-class excellence and to build highly effective sales organisations. She is renowned for her diagnostic skills and candid reviews of business issues, as well as the development of focused strategies that deliver results. Her track record is outstanding. She is able to prioritize and focus on the real key factors, rather than the common default steps that most people and organisations take. These key factors are the catalysts to provide each client with sustainable growth while keeping a keen eye on measurable profitability.

Commencing her career in accounting disciplines, Adele takes a granular approach to business that ensures measurable performance within the structure and processes that build firm foundations to support short-term to long-term growth. Her approach is applauded by executives for its ability to be applied in a logical and transparent process within the sales organisation, enabling excellent business decisions and opening the doors to unseen growth and profit opportunities.

As a public speaker, Adele is in demand. She regularly shares the stage with some of the world's most recognised business achievers and leaders, speaking with large audiences of CEOs and CFOs.

She captivates these audiences with her down-to-earth yet entertaining style and provokes thought in the attendees. As a speaker to sales teams, Adele provides focus and understanding of how to be high achievers and excel with new and innovative approaches to customers.

Adele is a substantive, high-energy speaker with the ability to provide insightful answers to audience questions through an interactive approach that keeps the audience engaged

Introduction

Before you embark on the journey through this book, you need to understand its purpose and how it was developed. *'Get Sales Focused'* is written for CEOs and managing directors of small to medium sized companies that need to take improve the performance and results of their sales divisions.

'Get Sales Focused' is committed to the development of the selling function in companies and, as a consequence, to producing strong revenue and profits. Written in a concise style tailored to the needs of the busy executive, it will enable you to review the information and adapt it to your organisation or role.

The purpose of *'Get Sales Focused'* is to deliver an understanding to readers of the what is really required to bring a stagnating or slow-developing business into strong profits and to assist it position itself as an industry leader.

It will assist sales managers to understand what will be demanded of them in the future. It will give executives a better (and much-needed) understanding of sales, this often-confusing area, and how to develop a great sales focused company.

'Get Sales Focused' will give the reader confidence to undertake the enormous and often daunting task of change in a timeframe that is realistic for business today. It will give you confidence in choosing the direction in which to drive your own company forward.

This is a 'must read' for both directors and sales managers if they are serious about building sales in their company and gaining a sales focus.

The content of this book is based on practical real-life experiences - not theory. It comes from thousands of hours of experience over the past two decades in consultancy and management, mentoring of management, and training; all spent developing the selling functions of a large number of companies.

This information has been used by the author as part of major top-line turnarounds for companies delivering sustainable results in just 90-120 days. The author brings over two decades of experience to this book both as a manager and sales developer and as the owner of a number of companies.

Many elements in this book may challenges its readers, particularly those with academic backgrounds, as this book does not follow a traditional textbook methodology. Rather, it uses the insight gained from the results of many successful 'revolutions' and from the development of many company's performances. These are companies that have enjoyed increases from 20% to well over 300% in their sales in just 90-120 days.

The philosophies you will find here are different: but they will deliver a major boost to your business.

Prologue

You have probably picked up this book for a variety of reasons. Firstly the subject of sales interests you or maybe it completely mystifies you.

You may be a director, senior employee of a company that has reached the end of your stress levels in battling the market place and/or the sales division and just want some straight forward clarity of how to pull it all together.

On the other hand you may be a director or financial controller that has identified the plateau or stagnation in the business and are seeking methods to bring the company back to its market position and with strong profits.

There will be sales managers who are going to read this book as they seek to understand or to simplify the methods that can produce results for their employers. They may be under pressure at the time or just pro-active to what can be achieved in the market.

You may be a sales person with career ambition for the future and want to set yourself apart from others to produce results.

There will be small to medium size enterprises [SME] business owners that are growing and want to capture or harness what it takes to be successful in business. You may be a mid market sized business looking to go to the next level.

We are confident that you will all feel satisfied as you journey through the book.

But firstly, you must understand that we take a different approach in this book to many others you read. The book is written to assist in how to address under-performing sales divisions where immediate results are required. It may be to overcome a stagnating or business experiencing a plateau..

In this book, we will talk about *'making money'*. We will talk about the real facts of sales force management and not the glossy or untested versions that people like to hear.

It provides a solid view of what sales managers should be doing in their role. We hold back no punches; we do not write to smooch the people who read this. We want you, the reader, to walk away after reading this book and know how to take control of your selling function and *make more money*!

The content is concise, it's candid. As professionals you take that in your stride as you are experienced in the real world and you know what you face out there on the battle-ground of business.

This book will take you through the full cycle of the past to the present, the present to the future. It will provide you with the information to make the journey and know what lies ahead for you.

Again, we are confident after absorbing what is enclosed in this book - you will go back to your business or office, enthused and armed with the knowledge and/or direction to make a significant difference in results.

Chapter One:

Evolution of Sales Managers and Sales Personnel

The face of sales and the management of sales people have changed considerably in recent years. Evolving to varying degrees, the area still has not developed with an overall consistency of focus and dedication of say the financial or production areas of the business.

Sales mystifies many companies and remains, to this day, one of the last frontiers in the management of a business. Known for its variables, it has been difficult to document it in any form other than the history of performance. Sales people are perceived as having 'the gift of the gab' and an employment role that has a certain lifestyle, rewards, and loose boundaries - not to mention 101 reasons for why 'it hasn't happened yet'. Traditionally, there has been no formal study preparation one had to do before going into sales, and there have been no apprenticeships: people just arrived in sales.

For many years this reputation and lack of training have meant that sales related roles have not been known for their professionalism. Companies did not understand or consider the impact - in terms of revenue gained or lost - that such a haphazard approach to this area of business could have.

'We could increase our business'... 'There certainly is more market share available to us' and other statements of that ilk are often heard around the boardroom table - but it usually doesn't get any further than that. It becomes a wish list to some rather than a genuine goal.

The worst aspect of this attitude has been that people have accepted the sometimes rather lame reasons that teams have not performed to projected sales levels, and why company returns have not been made. This blind and willing acceptance of the 101 reasons why a sales person, or team, or manager has not performed has not helped businesses. Rather than focusing on reasons why not, they should have been focusing on the quality of delivery of results without sacrifice. This is how the highly effective companies operate and focus.

A company's sales division should not be considered the necessary evil. Sales are not about filling positions with just anyone who applies, or working from 'gut feel' that someone is personable and seems to know what they are talking about. Up until now, the position of sales person/representative has usually been filled by default. The number of recruits that are not even skill tested in selling is quite astonishing.

The same would apply to sales manager positions. Many companies still view these positions as transient and of lower value than finance or production manager roles. They do not see anything other than talk so therefore they devalue the role based on what's presented to them.

Companies were and are reliant on tight fiscal and inventory control for their success. Some will invest in marketing activities to increase revenue but rarely are hard lines taken on those that contribute directly to a company's success.

The sales force is rarely accurately measured and reports are fiscal outcomes reactionary to what has happened and not charting how they got there. Forecasts are seen at best as wish lists or long shots. They rarely can be relied upon.

Sales is an area of business that is most often operated in the 'grey' and not seen as an area that can be systemised like other traditional areas of the business. But this is simply not true. Sales divisions can be regulated as clearly as a company's fiscal or inventory elements, with the precision of quality management.

It is well documented that companies like Xerox, have expended large amounts of money in the refinement of sales management and their sales people over the years; they were early identifiers of the positive financial results from doing so.

The refined focus has been phased in as standard company practice by other major corporations around the world. These companies have leading sales forces and sales management that are capable of sustaining and growing well established companies.

It is only in recent years that smaller companies (>$30 million turnover) are recognising the value of high quality sales management and systemised selling functions, and the impact that a highly skilled sales team can have on an organisation. Intelligent companies realise that it takes a finely tuned selling function to produce results. They have learned that it's not just about 'revving up the team', or having 'a better mousetrap'.

Once reliant on their products and on fiscal information, an ever-increasing number of traditionalist companies are now seeking to improve their sales forces and understand how to maximise results in this area. These companies are constantly in search of the ingredients and methods to define what the successful sales manager and sales person of the future will be, to ramp up the results they want to achieve in the longer term. In reading this book you become one of those executives pursuing consistent, improved sales performance, and not simply relying on tricks, gimmicks or worn-out methods from a bygone era.

A warning to sales managers. Parts of this book can be quite confrontational and should be viewed as an indicator of where you need to be positioned for the future and not as a criticism of the past.

To understand how to achieve your ideal situation with your selling function, you will need to understand where this whole area has come from. This will give you an insight into why you experience what you may be going through, or have been through, and how to avoid those adverse situations in the future. Sales Managers from all different levels will associate with the information contained herein.

Many readers will relate to these situations; some may even have been victims of these phases, while others will have profited from the exposure. All evidencing good and bad management practices.

One thing that is clear is that in all phases of development or maturing of the selling function, sales people have mirrored their managers. Their style is a direct result of how they have been guided and managed.

> *Where your manager came from in the past, will define where your team is going in the future.*

It is important to remember that the ability of sales people to perform through both bullish and bearish markets reflects their managers' leadership.

Looking back through the 1980s, a large proportion of sales managers that most people recognised were extraverts that were acknowledged for the ability to build motivation and hype around a sales team. Enthusiasm and drive were emphasized and the common perception was that the energy correlated to sales results. Turnover of personnel within sales teams was quite high and to mainstream business, sales was seen as a transient, informal industry.

Companies created an environment of 'try them' when recruiting sales people and the team was in many cases asked to emulate the sales manager in its selling style. This was very evident in commission-only sales teams. The sales manager was promoted for their own outstanding sales results and little emphasis was placed on business acumen.

In industrial or wholesale selling the emphasis was more on company loyalty and relationships with customers. The sales people were very much route or community sellers. They were reliable people who arrived at the same destination on a scheduled day each month to collect the order. They were personable and usually stayed with the company for many years.

Selling was learned on the job and in most cases, there was little focus on developing strong selling skills. It was believed that the relationship with the customer or a repertoire of tricks and gambits reeled in the order each month. Companies and sellers enjoyed the stability and they were easy to manage.

The influencers
Many countries' selling styles were strongly influenced by American trainers and their styles were based around the process of 'meet, greet and close the sales'. At that time, the buyer's markets had not been exposed to these techniques, so they were quite responsive to them.

This was the first sign of professionalism, or some sort of structured approach, in selling. A format and a process were used in obtaining the sale. Companies started to reap the results and the benefits of strong sales and a healthy trading market place were enjoyed by all.

The pressure increased on management as the teams demanded more time and effort to manage and educate. The smarter the teams became, the harder they were to manage.

With the changing economic climate across the world in early 1990, customers became wary and harder to sell to. Many were financially over-exposed through purchases made in the late 1980s and identified their over-expenditure with the sales people who had talked them into buying. Sales people were a convenient scapegoat. Many of the sellers became a liability to the company due to the preconceived ideas of the customers. The reaction in company management was to seek people who had a more genial approach to the business of selling. They identified with a perceived need to develop good products and services that the customer base would respond to without pressure. Companies worked vigorously to develop a 'better mousetrap' to ensure their competitive advantage. A mousetrap being their product.

The excesses of sales teams from times gone by were cut back to a very administrative-style environment. Rewards and high commissions were reduced to provide a more stable income of full salary and minimal incentive. This was beneficial to both the companies' financial forecasting and the security of the sales person. Companies associated hyperactive sales people with high expenditure and the more subdued product-focused style of sales person as the vehicle to the future.

> *Yet this approach is flawed: in choosing product over sales, many organisations now suffer as a result.*

There was an imbalance in the approach. It was not about all product focus or all sales it was an even combination to achieve results; a good product - well sold. The companies that took that approach thrived through the hard times and continue to do so.

What about the customers

The changes in the market place also impacted how companies thought about their customers. The customer pool dried up in a very short time as many companies collapsed, unemployment rose and consumer requirements slowed. Those company owners who traded through this period will remember the buoyancy of the late 1980s and the sudden shattering realisation of a total business slow-down in the early 1990s. In many cases literally nothing was left in only a few short months.

In the eyes of the surviving companies, the value of the customer changed from being a provider of funds to a highly valued part of the supplier company. With hindsight, many companies saw that they had created a culture of just pushing the customer through as a number and little attention had been given to customer care, a total contrast to the energy and effort of today.

Chapter Two:

The Achilles Heel of Sales Development Today

The past has created a culture and style of operator that will challenge many of the companies of the future. Sales managers will be faced with a number of choices and this chapter is going to provide information from a CEO or president's perspective of the choices they would want a sales manager to be making.

Sales people can also evaluate how they will move successfully forward into the management role of the future.

Sales today, gone tomorrow
The sales people of the 1990s are the sales managers of today and the future. Many sales managers today have developed by way of a product focus and in environments that are predominately product-driven. There is currently a fundamental lack of managers who are capable of both opening and closing a deal, simple as that might sound. More importantly, managers today have limited know-how and expertise to coach and develop their sales staff in the selling skills required for growth.

Many do not know the art form of making money through other people: the key that defines a good manager from a great manager. They may consider they have the know-how to make money but it's usually conceptual and not a reality. These great managers produce the revenue that all company members then benefit from.

The lack of people with exposure to a genuine pro-active selling culture that they can replicate in other sites is of great concern

A manager's ability to identify precisely why a sales person is failing is a critical skill. Many managers will take the natural view that it is a lack of selling skill in the sales person that has resulted in failure. Their response is to send these people out to sales courses. Yet a lack of selling skill is in fact the least likely reason for a failure. This typical reaction tells us that most managers are unable to look at the bigger issues within a sales management role or drill down on specifics to the depth that resolves the issues. They do not have an understanding or knowledge of what are the main elements of sales performance.

Old loyalties die hard

Through the 1990s sales people were strongly focused on building relationships with companies as outlined in Chapter 1. An offshoot of the focus on customer relationships is the managers' focus on relationships with the team and their desire for stability. The ability to be a team player was considered one of the principal qualities of a good manager. The increase of human resource based issues often imposed a perceived threat on taking action at the detriment of the company results and in some cases to all those employed in the company.

Managers did not lead from the front (nor guide from behind), but rather, stayed within the team. They retained the status quo of the company. The lines of responsibility and control were grey and the results reflected this uncertainty. This attitude is prevalent in managers who were internally promoted, as previous loyalties make it difficult for them to make the transition from team member to team leader. This has resulted in managers who are more focused on relationships within the team and on the longevity of the members within the team than on producing results. Results were sacrificed when the pressure was on to sustain relationships or company internal stability.

One of the greatest concerns in management for the future is the fact that many current and evolving sales people have not been exposed to a pro-active selling environment, nor have they been led by sales-focused sales managers capable of developing a sales culture and producing results through others.

As you will read below, many sales managers attain their positions through internal promotion, making decisions easier for their directors, and not by merit. A promotion of that kind does not generally have the longer-term growth of the business in mind.

Promoting people internally is attractive to directors because they are better able to control and trust a known quantity, thereby sustaining the current (old) mould of the business. Very few had actually been recruited through a formal internal career pathing process.

Directors communicated by this action that incremental change is acceptable as long as it doesn't upset the status quo of the company. They want better results without change.

Blindly reliving the past is not enough

Managers appointed in this manner do not necessarily show signs of sales prowess or management skills. Nor do the company management give them access to the learning. They lack the ability to convey the skills required to successfully open and close sales, for territory management, to run outbound or pro-active selling campaigns, to develop new and innovative ideas for business growth, to know how to respond to market slowing or where performances are lacking within the team. It is a combination of directors not evolving and sales managers not demanding to evolve.

These managers are in many instances simply repeating the practices and therefore the mistakes of the past, with only minor or inconsequential changes. This is not sufficient to carry a business into the future.

Some readers may already be experiencing the pressure of these actions and choices of the past. Managers are often reliant on the director's ability as an entrepreneur and visionary, but usually lack the skill to turn that vision into a reality. The vision becomes an idealism or dream that they share for long periods of time. The managers make few decisions and are in some cases followers rather than leaders. Some directors will have to admit quietly to themselves, that they actually prefer that style of manager working with them. The sales people naturally reflect that follower environment. The limited experience of these sales people (now on their way to becoming the sales managers of the future) means that the ability to make good decisions is sorely lacking. These inexperienced people are not well versed in decision-making and have no real reference structure to draw on. So what do these people actually use as strategies? They rely on product skills over selling skills.

The sales manager profile

The term 'sales management' has entered the language and describes sales forces ranging from one person through to hundreds. The role of this group is usually quite ambiguous in many organisations. Let's profile the sales manager of the past and, unfortunately in some cases, the present. Traditionally, the role of sales manager has been the least accountable role within a company, yet the most influential when it comes to a company's success or failure. In other words, this management role is conducted in the 'grey', with low real accountability, rather than in 'black and white' with high levels of accountability.

Many sales people naturally target the role and title of 'Sales Manager' as their ultimate goal, and consider it to be a career high. Typically, on achievement of the title, these people move into disengagement after a twelve-month period. This attitude relates directly to the transient nature of their employment. The easier the promotion cycle the less emphasis placed on the importance of the role by the person.

And it should come as no surprise that sales managers have the highest rate of termination/resignation of all senior and upper management roles. The usual term of employment as sales manager today is only twelve to eighteen months. That period is entirely dependent on the results produced in the initial stages or months for external recruits. And the length of the relationship prior to appointment for the internally promoted person.

Traditionally, sales managers attained the position by being:

- The natural successor to the position (i.e. the person next in line).
- A top seller who is expected to clone the entire team to their style.
- An extremely personable individual who is able to relate to all the unique personalities of the team.
- A person who creates immeasurable hype within their environment and is considered to be generating 'motivation'.

Great sales managers are few and far between. They have taken a different development path and do not usually fit the sales manager mould that most people would meet. They are demanding of their employers and usually are overlooked as they are considered to potentially 'rock the boat' or 'challenge the decisions'.

We have seen many times where great managers have been passed over for a more amiable recruit that more than likely will produce minimal results, if any at all. With this experience, it is not hard to understand why many great sales managers open their own businesses - usually in opposition to you.

Some interesting information came from part of a review of five hundred companies surveyed in late 1998 by Sales Focus International [SFI] in respect to education of sales managers.

- Only 2% had formal sales management training.
- Only 7% had owned their own business and were directly responsible for the business.
- Only 5% had an MBA.
- Only 15% operated under systems that provided total accountability in their role and transparency to their up line management

It is often said that putting a poor sales manager in charge of your sales organisation is like giving the keys to a Ferrari to a teenage driver... you can't expect to get it back in one piece

In past years there have been significant changes to the role requirements, degree of accountability and the skill requirements of sales managers. Successful companies are already well down the path of this approach. Their end of year results evidences it and the culture of the business reinforces it.

Throughout this book we will carefully review what is required of sales manager for the future and what executive can demand of them in terms of performance.

An inside job
What actually occurs when you recruit internally? Many readers can relate to the following example. Those that have fallen victim to this and those that have had to repair the problems after the fact.

SFI witnessed this style of promotion on a number of occasions. A good example of this style of management is that of a leading office furniture retailer and commercial outfitter that had been in business for a period of over fifty years.

Comfort comes from within

Phil, the director of the company, promoted Mike internally to the role of sales manager. Mike had a solid track record of eighteen years experience in the company in a few different departments. He had started work with the company, fresh from school, and his background and experience centred on warehousing. Mike did have some limited experience in sales on the shop floor, but had never been involved in outdoor commercial sales. Phil and his family felt comfortable with Mike, and the promotion was going to cause the least aggravation to the existing teams.

So what's wrong with this picture?
Stop here and consider the lack of respect that Phil and his colleagues appear to have for the role of sales manager, not to mention their lack of understanding of what the role actually entails. Consider also the hint of arrogance in the way this appointment was made, as if the business could continue, solidly on the foundation of past performance, no matter who took on the role of sales manager. The message here is that the position is in fact a token role.

A family business, the company had always been directly managed by the owner. The employees were reliant upon the direction and skills of the various family members to achieve sales. The employees had received negligible training, and the business had never employed a professional sales manager. Yet Phil and his family had been quite successful over the years.

Things slow down

The business experienced a downturn in a two-year period (at a time when the market place was buoyant) while the new sales manager was in his appointment. Although the downturn was obvious, Mike had no context, no reference structure of experience or training with which to counteract the changes within the business. Mike's only response to the problem was 'more product training'. He was unable to guide or develop the people around him, as again, his knowledge pool was limited. The downturn was not significant and was disguised by a number of events, so Phil and his family were not alerted to the underlying problem.

On inspection of the site, SFI found the following:

1. *There were no formal reporting mechanisms for the sales manager to report to their superior.*

2. *There was no reporting structure for the internal or external sales team to use when reporting to the sales manager.*

3. *There was no direction, measurement or record of activity of external sales people.*

4. *There were no records of in-bound or in-store activity.*

5. *The company had no marketing plan and no measurement of marketing activities.*

6. *The company had no sales plan, nor guidelines regarding methods of operation of the selling function.*

7. *There was no formal recruitment process.*

8. *There were no performance guidelines.*

9. *The internal and external sales people had no understanding of the sales process.*

10. *And at this point, they had achieved only $2.2 million of a $7.5 million turnover requirement after six months into the trading year.*

Basically, the business operated on the basis that everyone was honest and doing the best they could. The staff's good intentions were there, but they were not helped to achieve in any way by management. As the staff all had quite long employment histories with the company, they were unaware of how other businesses operated. New staff were transient and only low skilled or inexperienced people had remained.

Same package, different gift wrap

Phil's view of the situation was that they did not have a serious problem. This may seem strange but these occasional downturns are not uncommon in business. The directors agreed that a change of manager was in order, and elected, again, to promote a person from within to manage the team. Gerry had been the company's financial controller for five years. This kind of solution is referred to as a decision of 'same package, different gift wrap'.

The directors of the company exposed the business to a perilous situation in order to sustain the comfort level of existing employees. Gerry is no more qualified to take on the role of sales manager than Mike, and so the marketplace will move further away from the company and their profits will continue to diminish while cost cutting is also most likely to be effected.

Companies need to accept that sales management is a trained and developed skill area, just like any other skill that people learn. There are good managers and there are great managers. You cannot afford to not have the latter if you are in business for the longer term. They need to recognise the impact that a great sales manager can have on a business. If you are in business to make a profit you need a good sales manager working hands on with your sales team. You need a person with a proven performance in producing and increasing the revenue achieved in the business without sacrifice to the bottom line.

Many executives, particularly those from a product or financial background, lack the wisdom to identify the depth and quality of those skills. They have not educated themselves in what is required and their lack of skill is reflected into their recruitment practices. Many executives trade poor returns by pursuing the thought that there is lack of skill base required for the role of sales manager. They see it as a functional role rather than the extent of the human factor and sales experience to lead the people reporting to them and produce results. Producing results being the predominant reason they are employed.

To maximise your advantage over your competitors, you should be working toward:

1. avoiding the trends seen in many other companies, and
2. standing your selling function out from the crowd through high quality and experienced management personnel

In the event you are not able to hire the quality of manager you require, you then need to hire someone with the understanding that he or she must be educated and developed to the standard you do require. If that is not established before hiring, the manager will not undertake and gain value from any training provided to him or her.

The manager you hire will be the culture of your sales organisation. If sales managers are promoted internally, they will continue with a similar culture and only minor changes will be made. If they are hired externally, they will bring to your company the culture that they are experienced in working in. They may communicated a desire for change, but as you read through this book , you will realise how hard change can be and the motivation for the sales manager to change as an external hire is very low. Their background is your future!

The tale of the evolution of a company culture

Have you ever wondered how a company creates a culture and how it arrives at its current state? Here is a tale that will better assist you to understand the development of the company culture.

Start with a cage containing five apes. In the cage, hang a banana on a string and put stairs under it. Before long, an ape will go to the stairs and start to climb towards the banana. As soon as he touches the stairs, spray all of the apes with cold water. After a while, another ape will make an attempt with the same result, that all the apes are sprayed with cold water. This continues through several more attempts. Pretty soon, when another ape tries to climb the stairs, the other apes will try to prevent it.

Now, turn off the cold water. Remove one ape from the cage and replace it with a new one. The new ape sees the banana and wants to climb the stairs. To his horror, all of the other apes attack him. After another attempt and attack, he knows that if he tries to climb the stairs, he will be assaulted.

Next, remove another of the original five apes and replace it with a new one. The newcomer goes to the stairs and is attacked. The previous newcomer takes part in the punishment with enthusiasm.

Again, replace a third original ape with a new one. The new one makes it to the stairs and it is attacked as well. Two of the four apes that beat him have no idea why they were not permitted to climb the stairs, or why they are participating in the beating of the newest ape. After replacing the fourth and fifth original apes. All the apes that have been sprayed with cold water have been replaced. Nevertheless, no ape ever again approaches the stairs.

Why not?

Because that's the way it's always been around here.

13

A Real-Life Cage Full of Monkeys..........

Company Y had a long and established trading background on a national basis and boasted that the average length of employment for its staff was twenty-two years. (At that point we were confident change was going to be a big call.) The managers had all been employed from within the company and had progressed through the ranks, except for a couple of newer managers, Dennis and Richard, who had been recruited externally. They were not liked all that much, and people were sure they wouldn't last. Here was a really entrenched "comfort zone," or company culture, and we could see that the ability to defy the need for change was deep-seated

A fact of life
The company operated in a competitive marketplace where price was an issue. However, their marketplace was slowly deteriorating and profits were diminishing. The long-standing management had accepted the deteriorating marketplace as a fact of life. It was certainly challenged by the thought that taking a different approach could bring about benefits.

Management responded with the cry that "we've been doing this for over fifty years and we've done everything before. You can't change the fact that the market is deteriorating; you have to live with it. We're no different from all those other companies out there."

The newer management, Richard and Dennis, contracted SFI to model a training of their network management from a group of twenty managers. Their philosophy was that if the other managers saw tangible results, they would be able to roll out the training across all other business units for the betterment of the business overall.

Outstanding results, but they got stalled
The training was intense. It brought to the surface a number of issues relating to the skill base of the management who attended. Every belief the managers held dear was challenged, and emotions ran high. Reactions were extreme, and over a number of days, lively discussions took place. In fairness to those participants, they rose to the challenge and took on board the new methods and practices. They took them back to their branches and integrated these practices into their team structures. The result? The model group realised a significant increase

in business, which had them some 40% over budget in just six months! This outstanding result took dedication and effort on behalf of the participants, and it is no surprise that this group led the nation in results.

The other states were skeptical of the results, and their conversation focused on the disturbances to the old culture, how they change who they are as a company. Line managers were actually calling those involved and asking them to stop being so ready to adopt the practices because they will end up with everyone having to undertake the task. They could not see the results as a requirement, only the potential pain of change.

The reaction from the senior managers of the other groups was to opt for training from within the company as their best course of action. An interesting approach, and one that probably made a career decision for a number of people (including Richard and Dennis).

The management also commented that they were delaying the time until the training rollout because of high levels of work that individuals would bear over the coming months.

SFI kept in touch with the company. It in fact did not continue with any real development as originally planned. Basically the wind went out of the sails of the development concept. Only isolated contact from other "new managers" externally recruited led the company to undertake the training programme on pocket groups around the country.

From the employees: Richard and Dennis were isolated, and things are fine now—it's back to the way we always do things around here without any of those newfangled ideas.

Everyone can get something from this example. How your company responds is always the question.

Chapter 3:

Is Your Company a 1990s Company – Or is It Even Further Behind?

Do you really need to change?
Companies continually struggle with the need to be with or ahead of the trends. If we view the rate of changes in the '60s and '70s and then view the rate of change in the '90s, it would be best described that we are now on the express train of change. There is a need to identify exactly where you are operating and what developments you need to do, to ensure you don't miss the train.

In a research campaign conducted by SFI in late 1999, some interesting trends emerged in the way companies and management conduct their business. We surveyed thirteen hundred small to medium sized businesses from a cross section of industries. The information assists companies in identifying where they are in comparison to others.

Extracts of the research in this chapter will also assist you in further recognising the traits of companies of the past and will give you the ability to identify similarities, differences and areas for action.

Who was surveyed?
The companies surveyed are from a broad group of industries ranging from IT to manufacturing, with a turnover ranging from $2 million to $30 million. These companies are typical small to medium-sized businesses [SME] with a sales force. They are privately owned companies where the managing director has financially invested into the company and is working within the business on a day-to-day basis. The profile of companies surveyed is included in the appendix of this book.

Old vs New
One of the key features that emerges from the final report of the survey with great consistency is the need for companies to re-think their strategies into the new century. There is no doubt that past practices have been successful. However, with the ever-increasing global nature of business, the types of products and services that companies deliver, and the fast pace

of communications (both oral and electronic), many of the practices of the past will be redundant within the next three to five years.

A dangerous complacency

The current, buoyant market that is left over from the late 1990s helps mask many critical issues and is contributing to the delay in making the necessary transitions. In the near future, we will see timelines being measured in weeks and months, not in terms of quarters and half years as has been the practice. This fundamental change will place tremendous pressure on sales managers and directors, as they will be required to produce substantial results in very short time frames.

The SFI survey found that many managers, particularly those more schooled in traditional methods, are not developing the new skill base required. This is partly because these new skills have only become available to managers to learn in the past few years, due to marketplace changes and pressures placed on senior management. However, too many managers are not grasping the opportunity to prepare themselves, and their companies, and are therefore not geared to gain value from the revised skill bases.

Past practice has seen only very long-term change and development in business units, with tolerance only of low or incremental changes, which have been accepted in order to sustain overall stability in the business. This is the culture of companies that are extremely reactive and intolerant of marketplace changes. Only minimal changes are seen in these firms in this climate of predominantly reactive companies. These firms, which have not developed a true sales culture and growth factors in line with the marketplace, find themselves faltering and falling behind.

The gap widens

There are quite a number of glaring differences between successful models and those companies that can be considered just operative. Operative is used here to describe companies that tend to look towards their financial management systems or their products for technical improvements instead of finding ways to bring dollars in the door by going out and getting them pro-actively.

They have low profitability and margins restraining them from significant growth. The main distinction between the two styles is the focus on pro-active selling within the sales teams that characterises the successful models.

These companies make high levels of selling skill a priority and genuinely value their top performers in all roles of sales. Operative companies, on the other hand, tend to place great emphasis on product knowledge with selling skills as a second or even third priority. These companies do not value top sellers and sales managers.

Many of the companies surveyed developed from a product base, and the directors had either a product or financial background themselves. It is possible that this style of company may go through the largest transition needed to succeed, as they may recognise that they must develop new cultures and methodologies in order to gain a strong enough selling element within their companies. One of the key issues to address in this situation is the fact that many directors have not had the exposure nor operated in companies where high selling cultures were the standard. These people are therefore unaware of or inexperienced in the necessary basics to build sound organisations for the future.

The shady salesman of yore

When asked about selling cultures, many directors could only raise the spectre of negative stereotypes, such as the unscrupulous door-to-door salesman of the past. The notion of a selling culture did not, for these individuals, bring to mind any other, more positive selling culture. They were completely unaware of other models available for consideration. Many sales managers are unfortunately in the same position. Our survey showed that in pressure situations, they were resorting to product or financial action rather than sales action.

The following key issues emerged from SFI's survey:

- Sales managers are focusing only on achieving incremental growth through the comfort of 'closing current leads' and minimal up-sell and cross-sell.

- Little emphasis is placed on new business, averaging only 10%, which is reflected in the salary structures.

- Most companies have no real performance timelines.

- Most sales managers interviewed were unable to develop consistent strategies for building new customer bases while balancing the traditional requirements of sales business - a fundamental flaw in sales management today.

• Sales managers have a lack of foresight to utilising e-commerce for their sales growth.

A tougher market ahead

The market, evolving into a much tougher environment due to competition and economics, will force a solution for many of these companies. Increased pressure in timelines will see an even greater gap in quality and performance of sales managers in coming years, and companies will suffer at the hands of those managers who are unprepared for the developing climate.

Overall comfort and complacency; a non-confrontational style of management, even when personnel perform well below standard; the avoidance of difficult decisions; and selling reactively are, in part or whole, the commonly found situations in many companies. Why? Because it is the softest path to take.

Working a fully sales driven culture

Businesses that not only survive, but also achieve strong growth and profits are those that successfully integrate a sales driven culture into their firms. This means developing strongly pro-active behaviour, with an emphasis on the development of directors, sales managers and teams.

As the majority of managers in the companies contributing to this data evolved from re-active backgrounds, the transitions they made - and are making - have proved to be one of the greatest strains on the businesses that they have experienced in the past ten years. They are under enormous pressure; pressure that is the result of the competitiveness of timelines, the current marketplace and the fact that markets change so rapidly. Traditionally measured in years, timelines, as noted above, now measure in days, weeks, and at most, months. Nowadays, a year is a long time - too long - to wait for results.

Unfortunately, many companies will experience the change from a re-active culture to a pro-active culture through one of two ways. One way might be to experience difficulty in the sourcing of new method and management practice that can allow change. Many will not be familiar with what is required to achieve changes in acceptable time frames to the market demands. The other might be to experience considerable strain, with low financial returns and a loss of position for their products.

Late and forced change through low financial returns and loss of position of their product is usually unsuccessful change. The later the change process starts - the less likelihood of success

Companies need to start preparing now before they are under too much pressure and risk their existence

Proactive vs. reactive sales organisations

The following are extracts of the extensive survey conducted in 1999 by SFI.

Over 88% of companies surveyed were reactive in their sales practices. The single most common characteristic of over 88% of the companies surveyed was that these businesses are generally reactive in their sales management practices. A reactive company is defined as a company that does not conduct or monitor continual outbound activity in the generation of new business by its sales force.

Most companies showed some operative methods that indicated proactiveness; however, this was found to be negligible (under 5%) in the overall conduct of the business. These people report that their businesses are trading at acceptable levels in the current year, but also indicate that they believe that there is considerably more business available to them. They believe they have the capability to provide customer delivery for those potential additional sales—if only they knew how to snare them. All companies indicated that they are working towards being totally proactive companies. However, they reported that they had only sporadic outbound sessions that were predominantly in reaction to declining sales, and usually after one quarter to half a year of declining sales.

SFI found a disturbing lack of desire in salespeople to be proactive. Companies have settled for this complacency in order to retain staff; one significant factor that emerged was that the problem began at the recruitment stage and then progressed to flaws in management style.

Managers were accepting non-sales behaviour rather than recruiting better candidates.

Salary structures—do you really get what you pay for? The method you use to reward a person defines the level and quality of performance you will get as a result. This is not to say that all salespeople respond to financial reward only. Our survey showed that only a surprising 8% of salespeople actually respond to monetary reward—the balance seek security and stability.

Ninety-two percent of the sales forces surveyed were being paid through the system of 100% salary or 90% salary/10% bonuses. This method of payment predicates a person seeking security and longevity in their role. It is also manageable from a financial view point and causes no discontent in other areas of the business. A safe salary plan also predominates in manufacturing or those traditional-style businesses that were affected by market changes in the early 1990s.

Companies were reluctant to employ people on the basis of fifty-fifty or sixty-forty salary/commission, as they considered this would destabilise the team due to the intensive competitiveness this method promotes. Some managers stated that it caused discontent in other areas of the business.

I would view this reluctance as a lack of management skill in directing these teams, a result of the desire to retain secure environments instead of working with the rigours of the marketplace.

Sales management expertise. Sixty-seven percent of sales managers were developed through the company and only 33 percent recruited externally. There was a general reluctance to bring new sales management into the company, which, for the most part, only happened in younger companies where there was insufficient personnel to promote into the position. The decision to promote internally in this manner is generally highly subjective and is made at the cost of the real requirements of the company. These decisions are usually made as a direct reaction to the immediate, shorter-term demands of the marketplace and without involving any longer-term planning.

Directors report their businesses require an intimate knowledge of the business and industry for success. This sounds like an attempt to maintain a personal comfort level by directors and could be an indicator of their lack of desire to adopt new practices in their company, as these inevitably result in some sort of change.

SFI encountered an overall lack of trust in new sales managers on the part of directors, as they are acutely aware of the changes that inevitably follow such placements, particularly if the candidate is seen as below standard once in the role. Ramp-up time for new managers was approximately nine to twelve months, and many produced only very limited results in the first two quarters.

Over 87 percent of directors reported that they were not satisfied with the results their sales managers were producing after an eighteen-month period but were unwilling to address the situation! There was an overall complacency and very low expectations on the part of directors toward the position of sales manager. This attitude is underpinned as much by the desire to maintain a semblance of stability in the business as to the relationship that develops with the person, even at the cost of lower sales.

Sales management cultures. An alarming 92 percent of directors report what they consider an above-average degree of complacency in salespeople and sales management. They reported them as being very product- and service-focused, and many considered their employees did not attempt to close many of the opportunities presented to them.

Directors stated definitely that sales managers were difficult to manage in an effort to produce proactive sales forces. They reported them as requiring excessive amounts of the directors' time to produce management capable of achieving the desired results.

Many directors now consider that the lack of focus on proactive sales cultures starts with the sales management and extends down into the sales force, not the other way around, as has been believed in the past. Directors acknowledge that sales management is seen as a career high by many people and therefore constitutes their performance plateau. This is then reflected in the teams they manage.

Many of the sales teams studied were reactive to leads that had been generated by the company as the main element of sales. Sales managers accepted this, as they considered salespeople needed to improve skills with existing leads and up- or cross-selling prior to developing new business sales.

The type of person typically on these sales teams was attracted to the atypical salary on offer, which indicates a great need for security. The outstanding feature of many employees in sales team management roles today is the desire for security and to be "off the road," which is a major contributor to the complacency endemic in the industry. Yet, overall, directors were willing to settle for complacency in their sales teams and management in a trade-off for a more easily managed group of people on a day-to-day basis. This lack was accepted even when it clearly resulted in financial loss through missed opportunities.

Many directors expressed concerned over the lack of business acumen in the sales management people available. They cited this as a factor contributing to the tendency to recruit internally. The sales management people interviewed demonstrated a greater ability in crisis management than in the leadership of their teams. The outcome of this situation is invariably a lack of respect for the managers by their team members.

Management cultures. Above all, the sales management interviewed exhibited a strong desire to be considered part of their team with only a limited number making a conscious effort to differentiate themselves. Categorising the different styles of management as follows, the results were:

47%—friendship based

24%—dominance based, and

29%—professional leadership

The management in the first two categories was largely reactive to challenges and situations within its roles and did not produce results that exceeded budgets/sales goals. In the majority of cases, it was "management by crisis." There were no specific timelines for performance, and an overall lack of accountability was clearly conveyed to the team members reporting to them. These people had received little training for their role and were, by and large, internally recruited from within the sales team or organisation.

Of the 71 percent grouping (friendship and dominance), 18 percent of the managers had no previous experience in sales, and a further 34 percent described their selling skills as "average." The salespeople interviewed cited an underlying lack of respect for the managers and made clear their awareness that "poor performance" did not result in any negative consequences for the staff. Many of the managers appeared reluctant to make critical decisions and endorsed lower performance by avoiding these decisions.

Of the 29 percent professional leadership group, there were specific timelines and accountabilities evident, and these were communicated clearly to the team, with 89 percent of these teams producing the required results. They were, for the most part, externally recruited and had received an average of nine days professional external management training within a three-year time frame. Further, most had completed MBAs.

Results against budget/sales goals. In looking at the sales managers surveyed, SFI found:

- 31% of the companies were exceeding budget/sales goals;
- 21% were within 5 percent of budget/sales goals;
- 48% were not achieving budget/sales goals.

For the improvements in gross turnover and profitability:
- 11% had produced growth that exceeded 20 percent of turnover within a two-year period;
- 18% had produced growth that exceeded 5 percent but was less than 20 percent;

- 71% had not produced any growth and only sustained turnover with 5 percent variable. Within this 71 percent grouping, a staggering 34 percent reported a downturn in their businesses' results at the hand of a sales manager.

Full copies of the surveys are available through Sales Focus International.

It is the responsibility of the directors of companies to create an environment where the managers can evolve in their positions. The sales manager must be dedicated to the results and accountable for the results whatever the outcome may be.

Chapter 4:

The Business of the Future

Companies that want to succeed in the future will have to take a different approach and a different view of business. They will have to assign a different priority to the methods by which they manage their businesses. Many of you have seen first hand the outcomes for those product-focused businesses of the 1990s. You have seen the results of the finance-based companies, dramatically reduced in size, that have become notorious for cost cutting in response to the recession of the early 1990s. Both of these styles of operation are now suffering, unable to move with the market place.

Why? Those businesses that were financially altered to meet lower cost requirements excised two of the main ingredients needed for growth. These ingredients are sales and marketing expenditure. The old adage that you can't make money without spending it was never truer than in this situation. A company must invest in its sales activities if it wants to see a positive outcome. You must put in place well-measured systems outside of the traditional measurement methods of financial and inventory if you want to ensure that your investment is wise and to give you the ability to predict accurate returns.

Product based businesses are now finding that, from the customer's point of view, there is nothing to really differentiate one company's products from their competitors'. The customer can purchase a similar product from any of several other suppliers and feel satisfied that the product is performing to their requirements.

Very few companies offer a significant difference or competitive advantage with their product and if they do, it is duplicated so quickly by their competitors that they only have a split second - the proverbial fifteen minutes of fame - to be different.

How, then, does a company compete in this climate? The only real alternative available to companies today is to be a sales focused company; a company that can develop its own selling function through professional sales activities. This approach provides the essential revenue for all other departments to be successful in their own areas. A typical, traditionally organized company has five nominated areas that attribute to the company's ability to operate: sales and marketing, administration, operations (production, logistics, etc., depending on the type of business), finance, and information technology. In the majority of businesses, the last four areas of the business rely on the performance of sales before any of their activities become in any way relevant in the longer term.

They may be involved in the initial planning, but there is only so much a company can do in planning. You can make as many financial forecasts as you like, but you need sales to realise the forecast. And you can implement as many workflow and administrative systems as you like within the business, but without sales to produce the paper flow and the telephone calls that keep this element of the business at work, those systems are meaningless.

Production can only manufacture so many units before it starts to over stock. Sales must therefore be active to trigger and make relevant their workflow. And yes, information systems are important - however, again, you are reliant on sales to produce the post-sales workflow and the transfer of information in pursuit of fulfilling a customer need.

You can develop only so much new product, produce only so many units, set up so many systems, but at the end of the day *YOU NEED SALES!*

Sales define your success or failure

If we consider the importance of sales in the overall viability of the company, and review our company's situation in today's market, then we must logically prioritise sales in all our activities. The quality and focus of the selling function will define your longevity in the market place of the future.

The lack of respect for the role of sales management from the past is now changing - in fact, sales management is becoming one of the most respected roles within a company. Companies are starting to realise the value of the very experienced career sales manager who understands and can meet the market demands of today.

Sales managers of the past who have not updated their skills or have not produced results in the current market are not the managers of tomorrow. Many managers are currently gearing themselves as career sales managers. Four-year courses are being offered at universities, offering credentials and formally preparing people for the role. Real life education programme are also being developed and seen as a major source of information for management.

The mark of a great manager is a person that can make his/her services redundant, and what they put in place continues on and evolves to greater things.

The different views

- A sales manager with twenty years' experience in one industry is no longer seen as an asset, but rather as a liability, a blinkered person who cannot adapt to the outside world.
- The sales manager who produced great results in the past is no longer recognised - companies want today's people. And it's not about age - it's about current market knowledge and systems.
- The young, enthusiastic manager is now seen as a person who must have systems in place to manage effectively, as they have no real experience to contribute to the business and need some structure to fall back upon. Again, it's not about age, it's about current market knowledge and systems.
- A sales manager with limited computer skills or understanding will not be carried by other divisions. They will require the understanding to develop marketing initiatives and customer communication to define the business from the competitor activity.
- Business acumen is balanced equally with selling skills.
- Past conservative or re-active approaches will be viewed an inadequacy in a sales manager. Reliance only on product and finance will be viewed as a retardant to growth.

The following story demonstrates the different perspective people have to increasing revenue.

An Academic's Perspective on Increasing Revenue

The following is an extract from a report that was presented to our company in response to financial difficulties in an organisation during a review.

At present Company M is performing poorly with the bottom line that it is becoming increasingly difficult to generate revenue to support the costs of a large infrastructure. What I would like to do is reflect on why this is the case and what strategy can be adopted, once the short-term panic about the P&Ls subsides, to find a way ahead. In my view there are three fundamental reasons for our current situation:

1. Inexperienced personnel
Historically, we have put people who don't know what they are doing in a position where they can determine directions and drive projects. This is why they have failed.

2. Lack of commitment
Several projects were very expensive to produce, although we finally made some economies in the last two because of earlier experiences. They were expensive for two reasons. Firstly, the inexpert staff did not know how to follow a proper process, and secondly, we were unable to commit to an in-house team necessary to produce the projects at a reasonable cost, and so we outsourced a lot of work. This meant that key skills stayed outside the company. Worse still, at times we worked with incompetent service providers. We could not commit to becoming a well-resourced project and thus be competitive.

There was also a lack of commitment (or focus) around all product groups - all of the attention was being directed toward one, and it has not been given proper marketing attention, nor does it have an 'expert' to assist in determining its directions. Product 2 was not given much focus at all until recently. The new staff recently appointed came a year after it was recognised that they were required.

3. Staffing profile
The third problem is that whenever we had the opportunity to grow and take on additional staff, they were most often infrastructure, sales & support people rather than 'experts'. This meant that the fundamental problems mentioned in item 1 were not being addressed. Part of this reason was that a sales and support model from the publishing arena was being adopted. Consequently a profile of

the roles of people within the organisation now will show a high ratio of sales and support and infrastructure to delivery staff, which of course adds to the costs of delivery.

Now

Finally, we have focused on a core competency, but now we have less in terms of what we can offer than some emerging competition, and limited funds to make a commitment to that direction. In order to catch up and remain competitive in a fast-moving environment I believe we must do the following (as well as follow other areas of activity such as offshore ventures):

Sales & marketing focus

- *We need to de-emphasize the role of sales as being a separate set of people - this is an old paradigm unsuitable for the industry - a few well connected sales people who primarily function in a business development role is all that is required*
- *A very good website that communicates our value-add effectively is essential*
- *Put experts at the front line, publishing white papers and newspaper articles and meeting clients*
- *Repeat and new business will occur through the delivery of a quality product - so ongoing quality improvement is essential for a sound marketing reason*
- *There should be some direct advertising in journals*
- *We should engage in activities that make clients come to us, we should never be involved in making 'cold-calls' to heighten awareness - it will ultimately reduce our credibility.*

Alliances

- *We can create volume business through alliances so that the sales effort to gain work is reduced.*

Personnel

- *As this is a people business - our staff are absolutely critical to success*
- *We need to be seen as a place where there are 'experts' - and renew the emphasis on delivery staff and their activities*
- *All core skills in our area of activity should be in-house to be competitive, and be well-resourced, otherwise we should reduce the area of focus, and not state that we offer services that we cannot deliver ourselves*

- *Focus on finding and recruiting the best people - experienced people who can help us grow and develop in the right path - and follow an open, principled recruitment process*
- *Retain the best people with good salaries and other benefits.*

Overarching principles - conclusion
- *Hire experienced personnel - focus on experts in the field of activity*
- *Commit to a direction and resource it properly or abandon it as a core competency*

An interesting approach to increasing revenue but unfortunately has removed the core requirements to drive the business forward. An over emphasis on marketing and re-active sales behaviour and under emphasis on pro-active behaviour to take control of driving the business forward.

Chapter 5:

Shifting to the Future

The first sign of insanity is to do the same thing twice and expect a different outcome

To achieve any increase in a result, you have to make changes. The larger the result you are requiring, the greater the change must be. The direction of the change (being positive or negative) is only achieved by the quality of decisions and correct changes being made. Nothing can really overcome poor decision making when it is repetitious.

The selection of the changes is important and in many cases the defining factor to the longevity of the business. The error many companies make is they continually make small changes which swings the business to and fro and never allows the base to actually stabilise. They have no real foundation to build their business on.

To make changes you are in fact changing the culture in the business. A business is built up of people and their views and perceptions of the world, followed by the quality of effort and knowledge they put into the direction of those views and perceptions. The view and perceptions of the company will come from the ultimate decision-makers. They will prescribe which direction they want the business to operate and through quality leadership will draw all those working with them in that direction (without squashing the creative talent within those people).

To create genuine change you have to create a genuine change in people's perceptions. They need to see things differently on a day to day basis. They need to view the road ahead to be much more enjoyable than the road just travelled.

In many cases they will follow the direction of the ultimate decision-makers through loyalty and respect. This is the starting point of achieving change. However where no respect is in place then the likelihood of change is considerably lower. You will end up with a disenfranchised business.

With the importance of the selling function, SFI builds businesses on the following culture with our personnel and when on client assignments. This method is simple for people to operate with and provides very clear guidelines and intent in a business. It is a logical, step-by-step process that can, arguably, be considered too tough or politically incorrect.

But what it brings to our clients is a very focused style of person to their sales and management teams. A type of person who is capable of managing a business in the longer term to provide financial security to all those others employed in the business rather than a select few.

Sales forces are responsible for the securing of revenue that will provide security and growth for the company and for all members of the company

There is a high level of accountability, without sacrifice, in a genuinely sales focused business.

In the following points we will outline the five steps to achieving success in a sales focused organisation.

Cultural Shift Number One: *'Opportunity and outcome'*
As a first step, the business is measured on the basis of 'opportunity and outcome'. What and how much opportunity do we have for sales? Taking those opportunities into consideration, what is likely to be the outcome of that effort?

An essential step to take is the development of a sales plan. The plan is developed on the basis of activity and not, initially, on financial requirements. We build the plan in such a way that we take into consideration how much effort is involved in securing the opportunities.

The next step is to evaluate what degree of revenue is required from those opportunities in order to meet the financial requirements of the company.

Next, we measure the quality of performance of the sales force through the way in which they handle the opportunities in order to define the outcome.

In a survey of one hundred company sales budgets in 1998, 97% could achieve their budgets in two thirds of the working week - comfortably.

This startling piece of information is a very simple philosophy and can be a major turning point for your business.

Cultural Shift Number Two: *'Near enough is not good enough'*

Many company budgets are considered to be, the company's target figure, the amount the team should aim for, rather than the minimum performance requirement of the sales team. Therefore, when a company reaches the end of the financial year and finds its sales team has made 95% of budget, it is usually very pleased with itself. Of course, it isn't as good as exceeding budget, but it's not that far off, either. Some companies may even celebrate the outcome as a good year - a celebration of the principle that 'near enough is good enough.'

In our focus we would look at the missing 5% and ask why we didn't make it? We would not be celebrating the 95% that was achieved. Near enough is most definitely not good enough in a sales focused organisation.

It is all about being over achievers.

The third culture stems directly from the second and is the most important. It is that when we employ sales people, we work on a very simple principle that they have no problem in understanding:

Cultural Shift Number Three: *'Over budget is employment and under budget is unemployment'*

We have never met anyone who has misconstrued what we mean and have never employed anyone on this basis who has not achieved over budget performance. We write this into their contracts (whether legal or not), and those people who come on board and work under such a contract are 100% committed to being successful. Harsh as this might seem, this is the style of management that attracts good performers.

Those who are average performers, or the 'all talk and no action' style of operators, will never commit to such a statement and so you don't end up hiring them. This is no loss to the company as they are not the kind of people you want on your team.

Cultural Shift Number Four: *'The Working Induction & Procedure Manual'*

For success in the business and to reinforce the principle outlined in cultural shift number three, you need very clear company lines of management with clear boundaries. People need clarity of their role. Those boundaries define the exact nature and level of the performance you require of each contributor to the team; what is acceptable and what is unacceptable. The clarity of those boundaries produces the results for the future.

This manual must be put together thoughtfully and clearly, as it is an integral part of the documented boundaries. Documentation is essential so that there is never any misunderstanding, and so that everyone knows and agrees on what is expected of them. Sales people actually respond better in good structure, contrary to the belief they are free spirits and should be allowed to run free. Poor sales people reject structure as it can uncover flaws in their performances.

Cultural Shift Number Five: *'Small Business vs. the Franchise'*

There has been a myth, or philosophy, put forward to many sales people over the years, whether they were on commission only or received full salary payment. This myth was pushed at these people by traditional or out-dated managers, for the most part. They essentially asked sales personnel to treat their jobs as if they were running their own businesses. They asked their sales staff to take on board the philosophy that their income would fluctuate according to their own efforts and to ensure a high income, they should adopt the same commitment and practices they would if their territory or product range were their own. The idea behind this concept was to have sales people take ownership of their role, a very commendable goal.

Yet these very same sales managers gave their teams little or no guidance. They basically started them with a list of customers or telephone numbers to call and these people learned on the job. This is referred to as being deep-ended in sales.

This philosophy is rightfully referred to as a myth and only works for some 510% of sales people. They are usually the ones who set up in competition against you and do run their own businesses, usually after taking information away from yours. Ironically, many sales people are going broke in their own businesses!

If you review this philosophy from another angle, what you are allowing them to do is go to the market and practice, at your company's expense. When an untrained newcomer is thrown out there, they are likely to bumble in front of customers and present an image of institutional incompetence. They may walk past any number of opportunities as they are not trained or experienced enough to identify them.

What you are doing here is allowing them to go on making the same mistakes you learned not to make years ago, and wander around in all directions in the hope of finding the path to success. Each time a beginner reinvents the wheel at your expense, it costs the company directly in terms of financial loss and lost opportunity. In effect, you are paying a person to get practice in business at your expense, whether they go on to provide you with successful competition, or fail.

Those managers who use the old chestnut of 'treat it as if it were your own business' will often evince a marked lack of management skill in planning, accountability and responsibility. And this method conveniently provides the sales manager with an out - the opportunity to lay blame and justify the below par or non-performance of members of the team.

These points make up the philosophy that SFI presents to companies looking to be successful in today's business climate. These steps and concepts will enable your business to make the leap to success.

In Summary
To succeed, you do not need to disengage the concept you are aiming for, but you may need to approach the concept from a different direction. If you consider the franchising model and the success that has been seen within well organised franchise operations vs small businesses, you will see that those same, successful philosophies can be applied to your sales team. This is for both full commission sales people through to full salary roles.

A franchisee receives a licence to run a business, and is handed a formalised series of methods and procedures that eliminate the margin for error and drastically shorten the learning curve. This ensures that they achieve success in the shortest possible time frame.

Of course, this does not address motivation factors, which define the level of success achieved. Yet, over and over again, franchises are seen to succeed where many small businesses do not. This must be attributed to their formalised methodologies, the common point across all successful franchise operations.

Well-managed sales teams always have in place a method and technique of performance with performance standards to platform each person. This provides the boundaries and methods whereby they can achieve maximum performance in the shortest possible time frame. A good manager will assist a sales person in reducing the 'ramp-up' time, rather than increasing the possibility of failure.

A failing sales person is the direct result
of a failing sales manager

The tough facts for the future

The style of management that SFI promotes has no room for slow or poor decision-makers. In demanding high levels of accountability from the team members, high levels of accountability must be demonstrated by those who lead them. The hard decisions regarding a person's performance are made effectively and within considerably shorter time frames than many organisations currently allow. Too many companies drag their feet when faced with decisions of this nature. A one-quarter time frame must be the maximum allowance or tolerance for non-performance.

As part of the accountability, the manager must clearly acknowledge that the 'buck stops here'. The responsibility for sales performance sits directly on the shoulders of the sales manager without exception. Sales managers must acknowledge strengths and weaknesses equally and promptly and provide immediate solutions to situations that impact the sales results. They should not seek excuses or reasons for lack of results. They are pro-active managers leading pro-active sales teams.

When managers reject the philosophy of 'near enough is good enough', the result has a major impact on the business. But to do this, a manager must pay thorough and rigorous attention to detail and timelines. They must also have a complete culture enforcing the same philosophy or methodology. They must ensure that they provide accurate and clear leadership with immediate time frames for responses. They must work closely with each team member and develop them.

The sales manager role is the leader of the team and they must see their role as producing results through others. They need to know how to produce results through others. A successful sales manager will not adopt old styles of management such as dictatorship or self-cloning.

Through this new approach, which is a coaching approach, sales managers instill and develop the selling skills required in the sales team. They develop the culture and accountability in the team. If they are unwilling to accept total accountability themselves then the team certainly will not too. Their own selling ability is transposed into the team through professional sales training structure spanning over each year ensuring that they provide good solutions to selling problems in order to secure the sale through their sales team. They work with their team and their selling on a day-to-day basis. They are not theorists but rather good sellers with strong management skills - in other words, leaders - professional managers.

You understand and accept that, after 90-120 days, the sales team is a direct reflection of you

Not long term stayers
These managers of the future do not see their association with a company as long-term employment. They do not consider that achieving the position of sales manager is a career high in which to become settled and secure, complacent and reactive. They see the position as one that needs to be developed like any other sales role. They are focused on producing measurable results in a number of companies and on being recognised for those results.

Hunters and farmers
There are two styles of managers in sales management. There are the sustainers (those who can sustain a business and post an upturn in results) and the developers (those who develop a company's sales performance

above the industry average). The developer is more of a risk taker because they seek results and rewards for their achievements. They naturally install timelines. These people are the hunters of the sales world, whereas the sustainer is very much the farmer.

Who do you want

If we consider that sales people are a direct reflection of their managers, then we must also consider the impact of the style of manager you have leading the team. Do you want developers or sustainers? What level of growth do you want to achieve?

With the volatility of the market place and the pace of rapid change, the sustainer is a person who will eventually become redundant in an organisation. They may stay five years but certainly not ten years as in days gone by. Many companies have experienced the problems of losing a major client that is generating some 30-50% of their business. On turning to the sales manager they are unable to elicit a response to remedy the market. The ability to deal with a situation of this nature is not within their skill base or focus. Naturally the developer steps in and they will have to be externally recruited.

The developer (or hunter), with some skills in sustaining, is the manager of the future. These people will professionally grow business and are driven by challenge - no matter what age they are.

Hitting the sales manager's pocket

In future, sales managers are going to be paid on a performance basis. Not a performance package, in which they receive a bonus if they achieve, this is a salary structure where they are directly affected by sales team performance. We have seen this in commission-only environments, but it is now moving into traditional salary package areas.

If the company experiences a downturn under the new management, then the sales manager immediately experiences a downturn in income

The salary package

The salary package is made up of three elements. The first is the base salary, which will comprise approximately half of the salary package. The second element is the sustainable element. This is a figure that is paid in advance of the company sustaining its current performance. If the company experiences a downturn under the new management, then the sales manager will immediately experience a downturn in income. The final component is the incentive, or commission, which is the result of any over-budget performance by all sales team members.

In the recruitment of managers, companies will no longer be drawn to the person with industry experience but rather to a person with a performance background in a number of industries. A person who has worked within only one industry or on limited sites will be a second best choice and will not be regarded as a highly desirable candidate. Companies will value fresh and innovative methods and ideas rather than a regurgitation of industry methods.

They will try to move away from being sustained in the business' previous mould. They will actively seek people who are not blinkered in their approach, and who manifest the ability to seek, adopt and integrate new ideas. Many of the managers of the future will also routinely accept mentoring as part of their role, similar to today's successful directors, CEOs or presidents.

High quality decision makers will seek out this style of manager whereas low to medium quality managers will be most threatened by them.

Hitting home on the pocket

During a Management Training Programme with a number of managers from Company Z, we reached the section where we were working through the issues of salary packages and performance issues in sales teams amid other subjects.

From this point for the next two days, the line managers identified the need to change the sales team's salary packages in order to reward good performance and discourage non-performance. It was agreed by all that any new recruits would be employed under that method and the option would be offered to existing employees. Those who did not accept the package would be reviewed carefully in the future as concerns were raised over their dedication to producing results.

On the third day the managing director, Steve, who had been present for the entire programme, asked the following question: "If performance-based salaries are an integral element in the employment of sales people, then isn't it naturally an integral part of the salary package of the sales managers as the staff are a direct reflection of their managers?"

There was a deathly silence, followed by an outburst of protest from the managers, who were up in arms, totally rejecting the concept, and offering a number of reasons (sounded like a sales meeting to us) for their objections.

Steve had put forward the proposition that the managers' packages were going to be changed to reflect the performances of their own territories/states. They would be provided with an income guarantee for the first three to six months to allow them time to adjust and prepare their teams, and then the change would become permanent. After hearing their outcry, he went ahead with his proposal.

Steve took his managers' behaviour on board.

Our view is that he took it as a lack of willingness to be accountable and to focus on the sales results. Over the months ahead he took various steps to change his management team, resulting in a successful sales team.

Chapter 6:

The Role of the Sales Manager of Tomorrow

Sales managers need to have a very well rounded span of abilities to permit them to be strong contributors to the business. There is going to be an increasing exposure of their performance and accountability, and very little tolerance of non-performance by their management.

Sales managers will be hired for their ability to produce profits and revenue through all economic conditions, and will not be permitted to get away with riding the wave of success in bullish markets as sometimes seen in the past. Their skill base will be under much greater scrutiny, and reviewed much more frequently than in the past, and only career sales managers will be viable candidates.

It is worth reviewing some trends of the past in terms of desirable characteristics of sales managers in order to understand what companies aiming for success will be rejecting in their future practices and procedures.

The administrator
The years have seen a number of different concepts of what makes the ideal sales manager. Some companies placed their faith in people with strong administrative skills. This was often to counteract the perception that sales people lacked the ability to provide accurate reporting.

The thinking behind this was that if they had a person focused on administrative requirements, they in turn would force the team's focus on this necessary evil of their role.

The motivator
Other companies considered it far more important to have a person capable of motivating and coaching the team. They considered that a person who was a strong seller was of far greater value than a person good at process and recording. The bottom line to this thinking is 'if we can measure

sales through our bank account or invoices, then we know where we're heading'.

The product guru

In other situations, companies relied on the sales manager's product knowledge. They felt that if the team and manager were trained strongly in product, they would be able to design or communicate solutions to the potential buyers, realising strong sales results.

Regrettably, these three characteristics, while admittedly diverse, are all essential components of the role of sales manager and no one on their own is going to build the kind of sales force that produces the results of the future.

The sales manager of the future will be a person who accepts total responsibility for the role through exposed management systems that put on view their performance to their management on a day-to-day basis. These people will operate in black and white rather than the traditional grey areas. Senior management will not accept non-performance in sales managers and will be considerably more critical in their placement procedures.

Another significant change will be that their salary packages will be directly impacted when they do not manage the business into the required levels. This was once seen primarily in the province of commission-only sales people, but this will now also go across into the earners of salary package. Companies will ask their managers to acknowledge accountability far more directly through a salary arrangement that is responsive to their success or failure. This, in turn, will result in a natural sorting of those applying for management roles, and the gap between average managers and professional managers will broaden accordingly. Perceptions of the role will also change. It will no longer be seen as a career high, or simply as a situation preferable to being on the road, thereby winnowing out individuals who would inevitably become stagnant and complacent in the role.

On the other hand, it is also fair to say that those sales managers willing to accept these new conditions will be well rewarded. People reliant on practices from the past will not benefit from the newer, more generous salary packages.

Another significant change will be the measurement systems that business will implement. These systems will be interrelated and flow through from activity to financial in such a manner that accurate business forecasting can be continually achieved.

What will they want in a manager?

Through the selection process, companies will be seeking these fundamentals in all candidates CVs that are presented:

1. Sound commercial training and the ability to understand the impact across a number of business elements and units.

2. Sound decision-making skills demonstrated directly through a number of examples of crisis situations where they had direct control and input in rectification. The best examples of crisis situations would be those that affected the actual conduct of the business or its profits.

3. A proven results record in both increasing revenue (gross and profitability) and productivity of those staff members reporting to them.

4. Broader industry experience, permitting the candidate to bring greater experience and more successes from outside the industry to give their company a competitive edge.

5. A background in companies with proven management systems and methods, and the demonstrable ability to make the hard decisions necessary to produce results.

6. The proven ability to produce results in both bullish and bearish markets.

What will they avoid?

There are a number of characteristics that companies will be actively avoiding:

1. Long-term employment within an industry.

2. Longevity of employment within a company.

3. Lack of formal training in management practise from recognised educational institutions.

4. Career development within one company only.

5. Salary packages where they were not personally affected by rise/falls.

6. Evidence of resistance to change or coming from companies/industries that are identified as resisting change

7. Lack of professional selling skills that can be demonstrated during the candidacy process.

The interview process will be more thorough, and internal candidates will no longer be favoured, instead being measured against external candidates in a non-biased environment. (A career planning process would need to be in place within the company to ensure candidates could be measured accurately).

At the interview
The interview process will eliminate those people who are unable to demonstrate a degree of ability in the skills and aptitudes listed below. Claims by candidates will no longer be taken at face value - each claim will be investigated, and the candidate's depth of knowledge and ability to apply each skill to specific situations will accordingly be evaluated.

Companies will become more reliant on candidates being interviewed through professional recruitment companies by successful sales managers, and the use of psychology and skill-testing formats will increase dramatically.

A company's emphasis on the importance of the role is directly reflected in their recruitment process of this position.

If a company is to review the skills of the sales manager, there are a number of elements that are a must in that skill base. If any of these elements are missing this will result in a direct financial loss to the business. These are critical and not a preferential choice list of skills:

Planning - the ability to develop sound sales plans.

Analytical - the capacity to analyse the market place and sales performances/results.

Time Management - the ability to organise both themselves and their team and to prioritise tasks etc.

Financial Skills - a sound grasp of profit and loss statements, forecasting, gross margins, discounting (direct and inverse) cost of sales.

Selling Skills - up-to-date selling skills that are carried out in the market place for current validity. These will also include presentation skills and negotiating skills.

Commercial Acumen - perceptiveness with regard to the market, a mental acuteness and keen insight.

Problem Solving - the ability to identify and resolve issues.

Training - the demonstrated ability to train sales people to improve their skill levels, role understanding and application for a financial reward to the company.

Interpersonal Skills - the ability to coach, counsel, motivate and reward a group of individuals and take them on to become a team.

Personal qualities

In the area of personal qualities, the sales manager would demonstrate a high level of communication skills, personal motivation (always noting that people reporting to you are usually only 50% of your own energy level), the ability to lead, the ability to be assertive while sustaining diplomacy, and, most importantly, the ability to overlook one's personal prejudices for the betterment of the company. Executives not testing for all these elements are certainly reducing their company's ability to perform in the market place through the ultimate decision.

The day-to-day role and functionality of the sales manager is outlined in depth in further chapters of this book.

An important decision for a sales manager

Another problem that occurs when a person with such a high skills base is recruited is that companies always seem to want to utilise their high degree of selling skills by having them service a number of accounts themselves. This can be of benefit in some sites, but it pays to be careful - it is often a very poor decision with very bad consequences for the company. The purpose of the sales manager is to recruit and coach people to fulfil the servicing of the company's client base and potential client base. Where the manager ends up selling personally, one of three conclusions can be drawn from this scenario: either there are insufficient employees in the company, the team is too small to warrant such luxury, or they are unable to let go and make the move from seller to manager.

1. In the future, sales managers must make the decision whether they want to be professional sales managers or selling managers. One of the easiest dividing lines to this decision is the number of people that report to you. Once you achieve a level of six or seven people directly reporting to you in sales, you need to be a full time manager. We have always recommended that managers handle a few smaller accounts just to keep their hand in to the selling and market place. These do not need to be accounts that are significant to the company, just small ones that help a manager keep their skill base operative by providing them with a source of current, not dated knowledge.

2. It is important to understand that your success also depends on the degree to which the structures exist within the company to facilitate these steps, and the amount of information that the sales manager can access in order to help manage. It is the manager's responsibility to communicate to other management those requirements and ensure that they are put in place within reasonable time frames. A failing manager is a manager who is unable to establish the right environment for their own success.

3. The focus of your day-to-day activities will define your success or failure in the role. You must accept that as a manager your role is to achieve results through others. Therefore the others must be the primary focus of your day. The following gives you a guide to how you should allocate your time on a day-to-day basis.

   – Team and Individual Management : 75%

   – Sales Management Administration: 15-20%

   – General Tasks: ideally very little, but realistically, 5-10%

Unfortunately throughout the majority of management training programmes conducted by SFI, the percentages emerge as being the absolute opposite of what is shown above. Most managers do not spend anywhere near enough time managing people.

The development of the manager

The development of management styles is outlined as three definite steps. The length of time you stay in each of the phases depends entirely on your own personal ability to identify where you are and where you need to be combined with the information you gain to make the changes.

Traditionally, when people are promoted to the role of sales manager, their patterns of behaviour take them through the three following stages :

1. Attempt to sustain friendship-based relationships with sales people under the guise of 'working as a team'. This can cause a lack of respect in subordinates and will be reflected in financial returns.

2. When under the new sales managers' management the financial returns are insufficient, the next phase is 'dominance'. This is the next step in which the manager attempts to become stronger, more definite, with a lack of tolerance of the personalities and styles of subordinates. This creates a further lack of respect in the team and lower productivity and high staff turnover ensue. This behaviour stops the communication between managers and staff and the common, erroneous belief of management is that their problems have been resolved. The problems haven't gone away - the staff have simply stopped communicating.

3. The final stage in becoming a professional manager is finding the compromise between 'friendship' and 'dominance', when the manager finally starts to operate with clear guidelines and goals that all the team are able to understand and under which they can operate.

There are some managers that are caught forever in stage one and two. There are others that will stop at those stages for a very short space of time and move to the level of professional manager. The difference between the two is their skill level, knowledge, and maturity as a manager. Underskilled people that resist education and development are most likely to be held back at stages one or two.

Chapter 7:

Revolution or Evolution - What's Your Best Approach?

Looking at your business you have to decide is change needed. How quickly do you require the change and to what intensity. You need to map out exactly how you are going to manage the change process and place timelines on those requirements based on market place realities. This will assist you in defining which method you need to take of the two options available.

To bring about change in an organisation you must choose a methodology. Most methodologies fall into one of two categories, revolution and evolution, which we define below:

Revolution
This is the practice of bringing about significant change by overthrowing existing systems and methods within a short, capped period of time. Commonly, one would expect this to occur within 90-120 days and at a maximum, within six months of the introduction of the new methodology. Companies that have fallen behind or are under pressure require this approach.

Evolution
The practice of bringing about continuous, ongoing change or adaptation over a longer period of time, this style has no real time frame. It is more about evolving the business to a new culture and style of operation. This process has moving goal posts, which can eliminate accountability within the organisation's sales force. Successful companies can continually evolve as they move with the market.

The impact of revolution and evolution in your business
If you are in business, you will confront the question of what style of methodology to adopt at least once, if not many times over the life of a business. Making the right decision will define the longevity of the business every time. The choice is determined by the timelines within which the company has to operate in and its financial status. If the business is in

financial trouble or is stagnant, the option of revolution will have a much greater impact in remedying the situation than will evolution.

Revolution is not for all businesses - it is certainly not a practice all company management can endure. Revolutionary work is not something a manager should dabble in or the result will be severe damage to the business. A considerable depth of knowledge and experience as well as a unique skill base are required to effectively manage a revolution.

This book looks in-depth at Revolution.

A revolution is potentially one of the hardest phases for a company to enter into and one that should never be taken lightly. However, many companies could have been saved from financial ruin if company owners had a greater understanding of what is required and how to move into this phase. Used to revive companies and bring about a new future in the ever-changing market place, revolution is a valuable approach if done correctly.

Whether you turn over $2 million or $50+ million and your growth and profits are flagging or your company is losing market share while temporarily sustaining revenue, revolution may be a consideration for you after reading this book.

As a company owner, you are constantly faced with the changing world around you and the need to meet those demands. You have to manage through the maze of diminishing profits, increasing competitor activity, employee issues, and product and service problems. There is the ever-increasing need for the updating of information systems and production equipment, in fact, the need to keep abreast of new developments in these critical areas, and the need to keep track of all those ingredients that will continue the business into the future.

All these issues can be overridden by a lack of funding due to a lack of sales and sales development to sustain the requirements of the company

You may have developed the business initially from a product base at a time when you were personally responsible for its growth in the initial years, with a hands-on involvement in all the elements of the business. Over the years the business has grown and the employee numbers have increased. You have built on existing successes and steadily developed a strong business. It may still be growing, slowly, or it may have peaked and stagnated over the past few years. You are finding that the market has changed around you and there have been some subtle changes made based on the experience of those you have employed during your growth.

Those people around you have become very similar in their ideas and ways of thinking over the past few years, as you have all worked together and naturally developed a culture and practice within the company. To change the culture or thinking of the business is often identified as the requirement but the task becomes insurmountable as the correct approach is unknown.

The plateau

In most businesses there comes a time when most of the fresh, new ideas have been exhausted and the company has reached a level of satisfaction with what it has achieved. Managers may attend some seminars to pick up a few new ideas but these only have an incremental effect on the business and do not really nudge the business enough to develop consistently stronger sales. Current employees dwell on the past, on their successful experiences and sales coups, and are not willing to enter into a new process because they are afraid of change and the unknown.

Life has been good where they are

Considerable time can go by while each key person gradually comes to the realization that there is a need for major change. Even longer periods of time can go by from identification to implementation - it can be anything from one month to over a year. This is because even while a company's major stakeholders may have realised that change is needed, the decision as to the kind of change that will be undertaken can be a slow and difficult one. This is the time the company endures the most damage, as all action is suspended. Nothing is moving forward; the personnel are in limbo, mirroring their management and the market place express train is way down the track, leaving the company well behind.

Fast, faster, fastest

In business today, the market is estimated to be moving at a rate of change of approximately ninety days. This change is forced through the e-business environment and through the ease of global trading. Information travels quickly throughout organisations and the need for fast decision-making is accelerating. The customer world is now instant and therefore you are exposed to constant change and movement to remain profitable. The longer your business is in suspension or achieving only minimal growth, the greater the gap between you and your competitors and the market, the greater the chance that you will become a victim of the changing world. This is best demonstrated by the fact that manufacturing and other traditional businesses are continuously falling victim to the changing requirements of the new world. Across the world, these companies are reporting negligible growth and ever diminishing profits. It is instructional to see that the same pattern is being repeated throughout the marketplace: small businesses are departing, defeated, and larger companies are growing stronger through share acquisitions.

Many companies have still not recognised and acknowledged the need to revolutionise their businesses and become sales focused to ensure their long-term survival.

Many take a Band-Aid approach and in doing so, increase the chances that they will never truly embrace the change they need as they delude themselves that the band-aid is the change.

Taking the global approach - start a revolution
A revolution will affect every element of your business, even though you are focusing on the selling function. Band-Aid approaches or evolutionary approaches only impact upon the small area you are working on.

This is a simple indicator you can use to determine whether you are involved in revolution or evolution with your selling function

Company directors are often hesitant to make changes, hindered as they are by a reluctance to undermine their organisation's security of and by a tendency to want to safeguard their investment. The greater the change required, the less likely a company owner will be to venture into the phase. This leads to the actual decision-making about implementing change being left much too late - it becomes impossible to salvage a deteriorating company.

The decision to change is a difficult one. The greater the degree of change required the greater the impact of the decision on the decision-makers.

Some managers see the decision as an admission of their own failure and therefore cannot agree to move forward as they take the decision personally

Commercial managers understand that change is inevitable and expend their energy on ensuring the change is done effectively and for the overall good of the business. They measure through profits, revenue and employee attitude and satisfaction. They disallow any personal reflection of their own potentially perceived failure and see this as a phase of their own personal development and ability to identify and act on the requirement of change. Many books have been devoted to the subject of the impact of change on individuals; this book only ventures lightly into that area. The information in this book focuses primarily on the benefits of a change once a company has identified the need for the change, the need to determine an actual course of action, and how to implement it. We also look at the milestone of when a revolution will actually succeed.

Some managers can delay the change decision, and unfortunately some for a dangerous period of time. This can be from a lack of ability to identify when or to what degree of change is needed or a lack of understanding of how to go about change. More over the latter is a common problem.

It cannot be emphasized enough that the longer the delay in accepting this need, the more likely the resultant change will have to be comprehensive, involving a dramatic 180-degree turn in the opposite direction.

Revolution is a brave move for a company to make, and often the primary barrier to taking the logical step is emotion, even at the expense of the company's survival. Many consultants or change managers will not advise to go in the direction of revolution for three reasons:

1. There is considerable work involved in fulfilling the change requirements, with high stress and pressure levels for the lead person

2. Very few people have the experience and expertise to undertake a revolutionary change

3. Some consultants seek long-term assignments for their own job security.

Once you decide to go in the direction of revolution you must be careful not to make the task overly complicated. You must set distinct time frames and measurements to ensure you are progressing forward rapidly and meeting the requirements of the company and market place.

Without these measures in place, you will end up slowing down and working in an evolutionary style (evolving to the outcome than the revolutionary style in which it drives to the outcome in a restricted time frame). The lack of emphasis will also cause other problems to surface, caused by personnel within the company learning to resist the change.

The metaphor that change is like taking off a band-aid; you can either do it slowly and pull out every hair slowly, thereby prolonging the pain, or you can rip it off and get all the pain over and done with in one movement. Evolution is slow, and often painful, revolution may be painful but it's over and done with quickly.

Revolutionising your staff

Revolution has a direct impact on the company's personnel. Some will want to go with the changes and others will resist. Their own personal attitudes will define how they will respond to a changing environment. You will rarely find yourself making a decision regarding their employment; they will decide whether they wish to be a part of the new culture. Resignations are a fact of life during a revolution. Those staying are assured of employment longevity in a dynamic environment.

Through a revolution you will benefit in many different ways. There will be an increase in your personnel's productivity - we have documented up to 400% plus increases in the productivity of existing staff. There is a new energy in the business and a desire to be recognised for each achievement. The staff actually welcome and enjoy the tighter boundaries outlined in other chapters of this book and see this an advantage to their own personal development and achievement. The company thereby will enjoy a stronger reputation for product and service. Customers will benefit from enthusiastic customer service and people who are dedicated to the on-going development of the business. At the end of the day, both the company and the employees reap the rewards of increases in gross revenue and profitability.

However, it is worth remembering that everything new becomes old: if the revolutionary stays for too long, they will in fact become stagnant and slow, again necessitating a drastic change. A person who conducts a revolution is a person passing through your business. The need for a revolution may be recognised within the company, but the person who leads it will not come from within, nor will a real revolutionary remain to become a long-term employee afterwards.

Revolution is a moment in time in the life of a business and not a lifestyle for a business

Those businesses remaining in a revolutionary state are in fact a business that is out of control.

Smart management addresses the need for a revolution and knows that you don't fiddle with the concept. It takes depth of experience in revolutions to achieve the best outcomes. Intelligent management does not interfere with the process once it is underway.

A controversial philosophy
Sales Focus International believe very strongly in a fundamental tenet that is endorsed heartily by some, and disputed hotly by others. It is that, at the end of the day, people go to work to earn money. Whether you're the employer or employee, that's what you are there for. Your business or where you work is only the vehicle for making the money everyone needs in order to live. The amount of money you earn defines the quality of the living. We seem to forget this fundamental truth when people start wanting their business to be more than just a business. Some people want their organisation to be a community or lifestyle. The best company to work for is the one that makes the wealth and shares it with the contributors, so they can afford to have a lifestyle and community with their family and friends. A smart business owner knows to share the wealth in order to create even more. Inexperienced managers try to create wealth for themselves only.

Getting a sales focus
Revolution is about major increases in revenue and profitability. It's not about small revenue increases of 5-10%. It is about removing a product focus and working with a sales focus. It's about bringing major change to the business to give a significant outcome of financial and cultural reward.

The business must be focused on the professional operation of the selling function, first and foremost. The management must be dedicated to being a sales focused company. With profitable sales, everything else will flow on and become relevant afterwards.

A great product does not guarantee a result - A great sales force does

Revolution brings new energy, new inspiration, new methods and positive ideas. It has everyone working in the same direction.

Revolution is a springboard into the future for a stagnant or slowing company

Chapter 8:

Helping an Organisation's Selling Function to Cope With Change

Change is one of the most difficult things for people to cope with in today's world. People's past exposure to change and their experiences tend to shape their attitudes towards change, as well as their ability to cope with it at work.

If your company is very institutional in style, with long term employees, you will find that the staff find the change process much more difficult than a young business with relatively new employees might, such as a dotcom, which as a rule embrace change and see a lot of turnover.

A lot of research has been done on change, and much documentation produced on the effects of change in a company and how it should be implemented. In many of the sites where SFI has managed change, we have placed a greater emphasis on the outcome.

It is important to ensure you are not caught up in the change process, as you will lose sight of what you are trying to achieve. You need to institute definite timelines and actual goalposts that must be attained for the process to be effective. This is the approach SFI has taken, as the companies would not otherwise have survived.

Why is it important to put these measures in place?
Change, as already noted, is a difficult process. As a rule, people who facilitate change are taught to take their time, to carefully coach the people undergoing the change through the process. In theory, this is correct but against this one must also balance a commercial reality. What do you put first? The comfort level of people coping with change or making sure there's some money coming in?

The reality is that if you take the time we would all like to have to coach staff through this difficult process, you more or less halt the company's commercial activity. Revenue will dry up very quickly, and then where does that leave everyone? This is the harsh if unfortunate reality, and cannot be ignored. These two elements are extremely difficult to balance and you need to consider all the stakeholders in the change process rather than be passionate one way or the other. You cannot sacrifice the overall objective of the exercise as well as the security of the business for what is, in the end, a minority.

Our experience in change work has taught us that many people relate to the notion that enduring change in the workplace is very similar to experiencing the grieving process. The emotions a person feels at losing a safe, familiar work environment are no different from those felt when grieving for a lost family member or loved one. You are asking them to potentially drive a new way to work, wear different styles of clothes and live in someone else's house. These are all things that are naturally held as points of security in a person's life. In the office it can be moving the offices to a new address, changing the paper work system, a new computer and you have inflicted change on that person.

Their ability to cope with change is directly reflected in how they experience change in their lives. It is arguable that sales people can cope with more change in today's market place due to the volatility of what they deal in and the continual role changes with different employers. This is a natural change process they go through and adapt quickly. Those sellers however that have enjoyed long term employment with a company naturally find the process very difficult. From what we have seen in organisations, many times over, this would aptly describe the process of change in a sales force.

Attitude
In working through a change process, SFI has taken the approach that our only pre-requisite is 'attitude'. For any change to occur anywhere, the attitude of everyone involved is critical to success. Attitude will define the person's level of motivation and acceptance or adoption of a new environment.

Our experience has shown that many hours can be lost attempting to change a person's attitude, and often at the risk of losing some or all the staff who have started out with good attitudes. It is important to remember that in sales, this course of action is not viable as the cost to the company and impact on the other employees are too great.

The approach that SFI has found most effective is to lay our cards on the table from the beginning. We outline to the staff, clearly and unequivocally, what we need to achieve, and what our timelines are. At this point, staff take a short period of time to assimilate the information and make a decision on how it will impact on them.

Most staff conclude that they can undergo this change, difficult as it might be. They know that they want to continue to be part of the company. There are always a certain number of individuals, however, who, having gone through a process of evaluation, decide to leave. The prospect of the impending change is either too difficult to contemplate, or not in keeping with their views of how the business should be run.

These people have considered: "This is what we used to do, this is what we need to do; how much effort is there in the transition and what reward do I gain after the change has occurred?" Their choice to leave is theirs alone, and not a decision for you to make.

Basically, you can't force a change of attitude. It is the decision of each individual and they must live with the consequences of their decision. Your role is to provide them with clear options to allow them to make a choice. Your role is to be their manager, not their saviour.

> *People will often agree with their management*
> *that change is a good thing,*
> *as long as it does not affect them*

When working with people with a positive or accepting attitude, there are number of steps you must work through to assist them in the company's change process:

1. Provide the staff with a very clear understanding of the company's vision and, more importantly, of the steps the company will go through to achieve that vision. Do not read them the riot act. Take the time to outline to them what their involvement in the process will be. Ensure you do it in a very clear and precise manner, outlining steps and timeframes. Walk them through the process so that they, too, can see the bigger picture as well as the micro issues. The use of white boards and PowerPoint presentations can help greatly in this step of the process. In larger organisations, a

company document on the changes ahead can also be a helpful tool.

2. Observe their behaviour closely during this process. Body language will speak a thousand words. Their questions and contributions to group and one-on-one discussions will help give you a sense of how they feel about the issues at stake and what their understanding is. Those who just take it on board and sit quietly will need time to digest and make their own personal decisions. Experience has shown us that those who display immediate resentment or hostility usually do not last another 30 days with the company. At the end of this period you will be left with the core group who will see this as exactly what the business requires and move immediately forward with you.

3. Do not try a sales pitch on these people; simply present your company's case clearly and accurately.

4. Emphasize the need for positive attitudes from everyone. Outline to them what negative or 'behind the door conversations' will do to the company (it can destroy it). Be sure that they understand that people who cause unrest through negative conversations will be an impediment to the achievement of growth and a better lifestyle. The more informed people are, the less likely they will be to contribute to or instigate a negative environment. It is important to bear in mind that people will naturally fall in line with the majority. What you are doing here is setting boundaries for the business and to do so you need to establish a mindset at the very outset of your programme of change. Ensure that every member of the company understands that negative attitudes in the past are in great part why change is now needed. Most people have no desire, once made aware of the situation, to undergo an unsuccessful change process that is stalled by what amounts to a form of internal sabotage, only to face the certain need for change all over again.

5. Do not make the tasks insurmountable. Instead, present them in manageable sections, helping them visualise working through them. The basic KISS[1] principle of marketing works well in this situation. People respond to information and knowledge. Lack of information leads to fear, and once fear enters the equation, the

process can be stalled and unsuccessful. You, as manager, are responsible for their education.

6. Help people learn, but do not carry them. Assist them to gain an understanding of the step-by-step process that will lead them through the change. Establish their personal reasons as to why change will be good for them, and provide them with the opportunity to make choices. This means you are continually working with a positive attitude that just needs direction rather than ending up with people who are dependent on you. Again, the key is not to carry them.

7. Communicate to people that their skill levels are not a problem in the new process. Convey to them that you will assist them on an individual basis to ensure they are sufficiently developed to meet the challenges of their new roles. At this point, you are only interested in their attitude and anything else can be developed from there. Most importantly - make sure you do put in the time to develop the people. Training is the key to change. Relevant, specific and on the spot training for each situation that arises in selling must be made available. In fact, the more you micro-manage in the area of training, the better the results will be and the more easily they will move through the process.

8. Provide positive reinforcement where tasks have been successfully completed. Everyone seeks reward for their performance. Frequent small rewards (which need only be the positive reinforcement of saying 'well done', 'I appreciate the effort', or 'thank you') are going to encourage people to develop and reassure them that their efforts have been noticed and appreciated. Ensure you are rewarding what both you and the staff member can identify as a job or task well done. This process will assist in building a solid and positive culture within the company that helps people through the change process.

Do not underestimate the amount of stress and strain people undergo in the change process. Rewarding them will forge stronger ties of loyalty between them and the company while building their confidence. This stage is the most frequently forgotten, but in fact, the most important. People will not continue to perform if they receive no recognition for sound effort (no matter how small it may be from your perspective).

[1] KISS Keep it simple stupid

Who Blocked the Change Process?

During an assignment in which we took a public business through the steps to becoming a private company, we were witnesses to some utterly unexpected reactions to change.

The company's brief was to achieve success independently, moving away from having been a government-funded organisation. There were some 120 employees in the company, scattered through administration, customer service, and line and senior management.

During a briefing session to review the standards of service provided by the company, staff were asked to describe the standard and kind of service they regularly delivered to their customer base. Their response came as a total surprise: they described such extraordinary behaviour as

- *not answering nor returning telephone calls,*
- *purposely delaying action on files,*
- *losing files either intentionally or through sloppy practices,*
- *not passing on messages,*
- *not recording information given over the phones,*
- *falsifying file contents to read that the customers in question were satisfied when in fact the opposite was true,*
- *and the list went on.*

The facilitators were astounded and left speechless.

As for the staff's personal presentation - their dress sense could only be described as something out of a 'feral' collection. In summary, they appeared to have no sense of pride in their presentation and certainly none in their work. People walked in and out of offices and conferences when and as they pleased, ate wherever they wanted to, and constantly chatted on mobiles. They were without questioning the worst group of employees we had ever encountered in a business.

On being asked why they conducted their business in this manner, they answered that their management had never asked them to do it any differently. No one had ever said anything about the state of affairs, so everyone assumed that the status quo was acceptable.

Through a series of training techniques on the day, it was agreed that a certain acceptable level of behaviour in the servicing of customers would be established. They all worked in a team to develop standards and the information was shared with all 120 staff members in the room. In complete agreement, they enthusiastically took control of the situation, with a view to bettering their image in the marketplace and meeting the service standards they had devised. The swell of enthusiasm was remarkable.

The group set a date for review and it was agreed that on that date, the line managers would attend a session to go over any developments.

Come that day, the managers heard about what were remarkable efforts to change. There had been a change in the environment, with a positive attitude emerging and an ongoing development of their skills and standards. And the biggest surprise was the staff members themselves. Seeing them gathered in the room was like seeing a room of new people. In fact, some were nearly unrecognisable.

They reported to us on the new customers who were coming to them. In seminars they had achieved an increase from $1,000 in revenue to over $30,000. They were proud of their efforts and in return, we provided them with recognition of their efforts through the group. The dynamics were great and the business was set to grow and achieve commercial independence.

During the session, while someone recounted recent events (all good news), one of the managers suddenly left the room and returned with another manager. We were due to meet with this man after our session. In the meantime, this man, a largish gentleman, sprawled sloppily in a chair near the front of the room.

At the end of the session we proceeded to his office as planned. Once there, he proceeded to eat a croissant in front of us, spilling crumbs everywhere, and slurping on coffee as we spoke. He actually knocked the coffee over when he went to answer an incoming call. His conversation with his caller was revealing. He grunted, then hung up and turned back to us. In the meantime, he unsuccessfully blotted the desk with paper to soak up the spillage of coffee.

He told us that their customers didn't expect good service, nor did they deserve it! Everything was working fine, he said, they just needed sales, not a cultural change. He could see nothing wrong with the way the staff looked or their manner of operation. And it was clear he felt he should know: he had been a manager there for 20 years and prior to that, he had had some commercial experience (very little, as it turned out, although he referred to it constantly, as if it gave him some authority).

Well, in our experience, staff is a reflection of their management, and this really enlightened us as to where and how this particular company's culture had developed. The situation here was that the staff had identified the need for change and this manager felt he was losing control. His response was the only one possible for him: he suffocated that change. He was a master of control of those around him, and the net result was that the company then suffered irreparable damage at the hand of his management style and projection.

Without a doubt, a once-in-a-lifetime experience for us.

Chapter 9:

Don't Become a Delayed Change Statistic

Dakota tribal wisdom says that when you discover you're on a dead horse, the best strategy is to dismount. Of course, there are other strategies. You can change riders. You can get a committee to study the dead horse. You can benchmark how other companies ride dead horses. You can declare that it's cheaper to feed a dead horse. You can harness several dead horses together. But after you've tried all these things, you're still going to have to dismount.

What strategy does your company take with the Dead Horse?
Many companies struggle with the decision to change. It can take them time to identify with the need for change, it can take time to actually commence the review of how to change. By the time they are faced with the final decision to change there can be a lot of valuable time lost to the detriment of their business.

Many companies once making the decision to change will have the best intention in keeping the change process as a priority however as they process moves forward it is reprioritised as other issues surface. Most companies fail to realise that the issues surfacing are the issues of the change and are needed to be handled and continued forward to the ultimate goal. They are easily sidetracked and get lost in the overall concept they wanted to achieve. Some companies are steered off in another direction as the employees work vigorously to make the changes fit various pockets in the business rather than the total needs of the business.

Over the past sixteen years, SFI have surveyed and gathered information on companies that have been faced with the decision of 'making change' for the financial betterment of the business. These are a cross section of businesses and it was interesting to track their performance once the decision had been made to change. Various facilitators of the change process were adopted.

The one hundred businesses surveyed were from a broad base of industries and with turnover from $5 million - $30 million. These companies had all been in operation for five to ten years and all had achieved financial success for a period of time. No one would dispute that they were genuinely successful in their peak time. However, all of these companies were experiencing the beginning of a changing market, resulting in falling profits and revenue.

Identification of the need for change
Over a two-year period, this is how the companies surveyed dealt with the need for change:

- 21% did not identify a need for change in business practice or structure and without exception, these businesses failed*

- 47% identified the need for change but did not instigate change. Again, these business all failed*

- 23% identified the need for change and implemented partial change, continuing to trade (profits were variable and some experienced no real change whatsoever in profit margins) *(evolution)*

- 9% identified the need for change and made significant changes. These companies continued trading with strong growth. *(revolution)*

Failure is running at a loss, reduced gross t/o with reduced profit, merger, takeovers and closures.

Travelling down the path of change
Of the 32 remaining businesses after the first two-year period, this is how they fared over the following two years:

- 5% deprioritised a need for change in their business practice or structure and these businesses failed*

- 64% further delayed the need for change. No changes were made, as a result, and again, all of the businesses failed*

- 14% identified the need for change and implemented partial change *(evolution)*

- 17% identified the need for significant change, made the appropriate changes, and continued trading *(revolution)*

Failure is running at a loss, reduced gross t/o with reduced profit, merger, takeovers and closures.

A conclusion

In summary, the survey shows that the management of the majority of businesses were unaware or reluctant to implement change and that 68% of the businesses failed in the first two years.

Of the businesses that identified the need for change requirements, only one in four (21%, or the equivalent of 21 companies from the original review group) actually made those changes. These strategies extended their profitability by a further two plus years.

Conclusion

- Of those companies that identified the need to change and deferred the time frame to commence, only 15 used revolution as their change process. Twenty-seven of these companies used evolution. Over 50% of the companies failed due to poor decision making on the part of their executives.

- The average company took twelve to fifteen months to identify the need for change.

- Those companies that deferred change for six to twelve months were actually driven into starting change (evolution or revolution) when they:

    - Lost market share and/or major contracts

    - Experienced a downturn in the financial status of their company for a period of more than two years

    - Lost product lines and diversification

- Successful companies took up to four months to get started in either the evolution or revolution process from the time of identification.

- Staff lost interest in the change process in less than six months from the time of the announcement that change would be implemented.

- Management lost interest in a quarter where no real results were being achieved.

Who's driving the change

Other trends emerged from the survey results when SFI looked at why companies avoid change, what the impact on personnel was, and how successful change implementation works.

- Change by external consultants or a totally dedicated full time contracted internal team achieved a success rate of 79%

- Change driven by the company management trained in change techniques achieved a success rate of 30% over an average time of 2.1 years.

- Change by existing company management resulted in a success rate of 18% in 2.9 years

- Change conducted by the employees - not measured

So what stopped the change process
The most common barriers to change were cited as:

- A lack of understanding of the real effects on the business and a reliance on past success

- Executives who are not sure where to begin, and who do not understand how to make the right choices

- Executives who are not sales people themselves and do not understand the complexity of the work needed to raise sales levels

- Conflict between internal divisions to get the project underway

- Executives or line managers who dread the loss of their jobs or privileged positions

- Executives who still perceive the company as successful and are unable to see that there is any need for change

- There were more important projects that required existing resources and time

- Employees who were not comfortable with change

- A perception that the company still had a comfortable market share and viability from past success

- A focus on electronic/administration process over customer process

- Time and money - daily tasks kept them inwardly focused.

Suffering existing woes is sometimes thought to be much easier than enduring change, even if the change is for better financial results

Chapter 10:

Decision Makers Who Do Make a Difference

The ability to make decisions and, furthermore, good decisions, is one of the great challenges - and goals - for all leaders. A leader is per se a decision-maker, and people are not only recognised for their decision-making skills; they are also measured by how consistently they make good decisions.

Every day people are faced with making decisions. They can range from 'Do I purchase full or skim milk?' through to 'Should I change the structure of the entire division?' The level of decision-making you experience relates directly to your role in the company. All company hierarchies are based on decision-making ability, with the decisions resulting in the greatest ramifications for a company, involving the most money, taking place at the top of the corporate ladder. There is a major difference between the decisions made by the CEO vs those made by the sales person. However, as a law of nature and business, people find that everyone is very quick to offer advice on the decision you should be making, regardless of what level you are at.

Decision-making is a skill like any other skill. It needs to be understood, learned, practiced and perfected to the best of any individual's personal ability. Those around you will judge the level you have achieved by the roles they give you within the company.

There are a number of important ingredients to good decision-making:

1. A good decision will only come from fact and never hearsay. Always review your situation and ensure you are responding to a factual situation.

2. Becoming a good decision-maker is about taking risks, risks that can expose you both as being wise or just plain incompetent in your work. Decision-makers do not make foolhardy decisions, but they do take risks - risks that are calculated and experience based.

3. When a bad or poor decision is made, your reaction should not be panic or a justification of the failure. It must be about focusing not so much on the decision you just made, but on how quickly you analyse the situation and act with a response that involves a better decision to rectify the situation. You will then be judged not so much on the poor decision but on how you acknowledged it and remedied it. However, if you have a track record of frequent bad decisions, there is a form of forgiveness that will not apply. Forgiveness wears thin.

At a seminar in Australia where General Schwarzkopf was one of the speakers (following his successful control of the Gulf War situation), he confirmed that you can only know if a decision is a good decision in hindsight. At the time it may seem right but the hindsight will advise whether you were correct or not.

A quality statement and one that should be remembered.

In business you are constantly making decisions with sales forces. They can range from small decisions to major decisions. As a sales manager you are always being asked, for example, if a particular customer can be given some sort of benefit or discount, of if there can be a change in their terms, what to charge them in specific situations, or whether a representative should attend a location - the list goes on. Combined with those smaller, day-to-day decisions are questions that will impact the business in a more significant way. These will be questions regarding how a sales person approaches certain new business, what information should be in proposals, whether product lines should be focused upon. Then there are the really major decisions such as business direction, product mix, marketing content, human resources-related decisions.

Business is about the constant making of decisions; small decisions on day-today activities and major decisions that will affect the direction and success of the company. As a sales manager, these skills must be well honed and based on experience. Risks should be calculated, not taken heedlessly, with no thought as to past experience or future consequences. You can have an enormous influence on your company and how it is perceived in the market place.

If we were to review what we would consider the qualities of a great decision-maker they would include:

- The ability to make commercial decisions at all times.
- The capacity to make those decisions within reasonable time frames on a consistent basis.
- Being able to respond to any given situation within 24 hours and to make a calculated and commercial decision for the betterment of the business.

These are the kind of people that employees will willingly follow and actually seek out as their mentors and management. Staff gain confidence in the abilities of these kind of people and are able to trust their outcomes.

As a manager you need to be able to identify your own decision-making ability in order to be able to improve or expand it. To gain an understanding of your skill level, below is a useful series of questions you may wish to ask yourself:

- How often do you make business decisions?
- At what level are those decisions?
- How many other people are affected by your decisions?
- In hindsight, how many of your decisions have been good?
- Is there a level of decision-making where you start to make errors of judgment?
- How quickly do you respond to making decisions?
- Are you continually reliant on others' input to make decisions?

If we analyse why some people are capable of making great decisions and others' decisions are questionable, two contributing factors clearly emerge.

The first factor is the personality profile of the person. Some people are naturally drawn to making decisions and others are inclined to delay making a decision. This is a personal characteristic that can be hard to change, but can be changed if the individual is prepared to put in the work to do so.

The second factor is your experience in business and life in general. The more you have experienced, the more skilled you will have in the art of decision-making.

The following breakdown will provide you with a guide to the decision-making process as experienced by individuals under pressure.

Immediate decision makers

These people are very confident and view each situation from a commercial standpoint 99% of the time. They are direct and to the point and interested in the bottom line and how it progresses the company or resolves the situation. They do not like being placed in a situation where they have no choices other than yes or no. They are best when there are alternate choices to make a decision.

Their decision-making process is quite short and deliberate. They will naturally take control and usually have a more extensive decision-making experience than other individuals. They are naturally motivated to lead, and enjoy the decision-making process.

Spontaneous decision makers

These people dislike being under pressure and will continually make decisions to avoid pressure situations. The decisions will be spontaneous and in response to the situation. In many cases a number of decisions will be made, constantly changing the overall direction in which the business or team is heading. These individuals are vulnerable and responsive to emotional situations and prefer - and actively seek - a playful and relaxed environment. They are inclined to sweep situations under the carpet by not giving sufficient weight to difficult situations.

Like their designation, their decisions are quite rapid and spontaneous. They are prone to make decisions that will stand them out from the crowd or try new and eventful methods of business.

Thoughtful decision makers

These people take time to make decisions. They carefully review all the options and consider the impact of any decision before making their final choice. They will research subjects thoroughly and seek as much information as possible. Quite often the research task far surpasses the size of the decision actually being made. They have no sense of time as a restricting factor, so the critical moment can pass without a decision being made, with the end result that the opportunity is lost. These people may use rational thought and reasoning - they're just too cautious to be decisive.

Once a decision has been made, they do not generally change their mind unless placed under extreme pressure to do so. And even then, they may well not.

Emotion-based decision maker

Emotion-based decision-makers are very concerned over the personal impact of decisions on those people around them. They will delay or avoid making decisions that may cause a negative or upsetting impact on others. They place the highest emphasis on relationships rather than on the business. They naturally have a tendency to want to nurture those around them.

They are inclined to take and seek collaborative decisions to ensure the stability of relationships with those they work with, rather than risk making a sound decision that renders them unpopular and upsets the group. They do not like taking risks are most likely to follow the actions of others in business or competition.

It is important to remember that all great decision-makers are respected - but not necessarily liked at the time.

Chapter 11:

Putting in the Foundations for a Revolution or Starting a New Role in Sales Management

If you are starting in a sales management role, these are the fundamental steps that must be taken. If you are an executive considering the options of becoming a sales focused organisation then you also will be reviewing this chapter in depth.

If you have made the decision to take your business on the route of a revolution, there are some fundamental strategies that must be put in place first. The steps for an evolution are similar to these, but there is no pressure of time involved.

Decision One

The most critical decision with any revolution is who is going to be the leader? This person will define the success or failure of your development. It is strongly recommended that an external person be used as an internal or current member of the company will not be able to command the same level of control and respect. They will be challenged by all in the company and are often rejected by fellow employees including other management. When you promote a person to the role from within there is always discontent in the ranks and personnel actively resent that person. An external and independent person is seen as exactly that - external and independent.

There are a number of issues that you must consider carefully.

Firstly, precisely what experience does the person have? Are you satisfied that this person meets all your requirements and more, and have you verified all of this person's claims? Is this person proven, with effective results in short time frames? If the results they have produced in the past have happened over a twelve-month plus period of time, then this is not the person for the role.

Secondly, once you are satisfied that this person has the background and experience, are you convinced that this person has the intestinal fortitude to go the distance with the revolution, no matter how bad it gets? Can this person last the distance and maintain the strategies that have been decided upon?

Thirdly - what about this person's remuneration? And what makes this person want to carry out such a stressful and arduous task? Ask yourself "why would they continue through the good or the bad?" What is their motivation and are you meeting those requirements with the assignment?

Be warned, these people are not going to be cheap to contract, but the results will certainly offset any costs involved. A wise remuneration agreement will be results -based, with some foundation payments also involved.

Decision Two

The next critical decision you must make is 'are all the key players 100% dedicated to the outcome too?'

Firstly, let's clarify who the key players are. These are the major decision makers; the people with the most influence on the business, and include national managers, general managers and divisional managers.

These people need to be carefully reviewed for their own performance under pressure and the ability of the company to work through stressful or change periods. Have they successfully been a part of change in the past, or is their first experience of major change? Many managers can give their CEO the answers they want to hear, but under pressure they will work vigorously to revert the business to its previous form.

If your key people are only paying lip service to the concept you are trying to implement, the revolution process is at risk of ultimately failing. Our experience is that this 'quiet opposition' actually will surface in approximately weeks six to eight of a 120-day turnaround.

Such a failure means that your business will join the ranks of the multitude of other companies that have attempted something and failed. This is because, instead of ensuring change can be made, they have actually trained their personnel to improve their change-resistance skill bases rather than to accept change and thereby achieve results.

You're either on board or over board

Some companies have to make tough decisions from the very beginning by removing key people who are in a position to halt the change, and are likely to do so. Unless a company takes a good, hard look at these people and makes the appropriate decisions, it is likely to stop its success. Many of the CEOs we have dealt with have encountered this attitude in their people.

Who's putting who overboard

SFI witnessed a scenario with senior management in a company several years ago, that has always remained on our minds.

A computer industry company approached us regarding sales development plans for their organisation. The decision makers included the Managing Director - Peter, Financial Controller - Trevor, and Commercial Manager - Howard.

Howard was responsible for the sales results that were at best losing approx. 10% off the previous months level, every month for eight months. The business had employed new sales personnel to boost sales and their impact was non-existent in the figures. Howard was most uncomfortable with the situation of external consultants in the business and aired his thoughts openly.

Peter was aware that significant changes were needed and a new approach to the market and sales would be the only saviour to stop this on-going downturn. Trevor was in agreement at all times. He was in fact a primary driver in the project being undertaken.

After working through the review process and identifying all the problems that required rectification, Peter was far from impressed with the situation that Howard had traded them into. They were in unnecessary financial pressure. Peter decided a clean slate was required and removed Howard from the company.

This move was not appreciated by Trevor as he was quite friendly with Howard, even though he had failed to perform in his role. In an extraordinary move Trevor went to the other directors of the company and had Peter removed as Managing Director. Trevor achieved in getting the role for himself (and then went on a two week vacation).

So who was on-board or over-board. You can imagine the sales development was very deprioritised with all this executive shuffling going on.

Onward the revolution

Well-researched and calculated decisions must be behind these two very critical decisions. Once they are in place, you must start to move forward with the revolution.

Behind the scenes
Before announcing what is planned to the company, or to any personnel, there are a number of steps that you must take as the leader of the revolution.

You will need to carefully review where the business is operating at this point and identify how much is involved in bringing it to the required level. It can be difficult to identify these points and experience will show you where to look for the indicators. A sound rule of thumb is 'what ever you find, double it and you'll be close to heart of the company's problems'.

Reviewing
You should allow only two weeks for the review process. You are reviewing facts and excluding any emotional issues. You must avoid becoming caught up in the culture and in why the necessary change has not happened in the past. Evaluate past results and, based on your own experience, you will be able to identify what has gone wrong.

In many cases you will find the management and staff have engaged in a number of conceptually sound activities, however, on closer inspection, you will realise that they lacked the depth of skill and wisdom to actually manage themselves to a profitable fruition.

It is important to understand exactly where the sales force is coming from, and what exactly is their view of the world. Do not start the association by telling them what they should have been or should now be doing.

Twelve month plans
Have the sales and marketing people develop simple plans for the coming twelve months. Give them a brief outline of what the content should be but do not guide them. The idea is to provide them with a framework only. This will test their abilities and give you clear evidence of the style and skill base of each and every person you are dealing with.

The purpose of this exercise is to determine where they are coming from and not to lead them in any particular direction. Provide them with a deadline for the return of the plans to you and ensure they clearly understand that their employment is not under threat. Let them know that what you are doing is seeking their input into how the business is currently operating.

Once a plan is returned, organize for a one-on-one review session with each person. Go over the plan in detail with them and have them explain why they are taking the course of action outlined. Review their customer interaction and analyse them carefully as a contributing member of the team. How much are they contributing in revenue, profit, forecasting, skill, and knowledge?

Most importantly, assess their attitude. You can determine how they fit into the overall scope of the team and, importantly, how they fit into the overall plan of where the business needs to be. In this way, you will be able to identify what skilling and assistance they will require to operate at your required levels. At the end of the day the priority in retaining any team member is going to be ATTITUDE.

On completion of this two-week phase you will know exactly what steps are required to be taken. In some locations you will find that people will resign before you even start. Experience shows that these are the people who have been enjoying a great non-contributing lifestyle, or playing games in the business, and they know their time has come to an end. They jump ship before it starts to leave the dock.

Where does everyone fit in?

At this point, your review process will permit you to identify which personnel are going to be long term prospects for the business, which personnel are better suited to other roles, and who is likely to leave once the new systems are put into place.

Sometimes the very tough decision to terminate a person's employment must be made in the start-up stages. Only experienced revolutionists can identify this need. What people find when they embark on this course of action is that the people leave once they are aware of the journey ahead of them. There is very rarely the need to actually terminate a person.

The simplest approach in any company would be to terminate all existing staff and start all over again afresh. However, this is not necessarily the most effective and common sense approach. The company will only learn from the development of existing staff rather than starting with a new group and repeating many of the mistakes of the past.

A little bit of knowledge is a dangerous thing

However, a lot of knowledge is very useful. From this point you will be identifying what other resources you will require to complete the development. These are the elements missing from the business that have to be sourced from outside.

Be very careful not to leak details of what you are intending to do or the company rumour-mill (and every company has one, don't be lulled into thinking otherwise!) will have the project well out of balance and away from the direction you want to take before you even start. It will unnecessarily cause people to throw up barriers as they will be acting on inadequate or incorrect information.

Don't underestimate the value of a counsellor

During the process there are naturally a lot of toes stepped on, people who take offence at things that one would least expect. The organisation will become quite tender to situations going on around them. It is important that you have a person working with you who can assist as a counsellor. To take the role yourself will detract from the task at hand and considerably slow down the time frames for completion of the work.

The actions of the revolution can impact people in every corner of the business; it can impact decision-makers in the company even more as they are attacked on all quarters by personnel challenging their decision. A counsellor can be a person in the business who has good tactic and people skills or it can be someone recruited externally (with commercial experience in these environments) to work through the issues.

Not a problem, this will not affect you.

Whilst working in a revolution assignment, we heard an amusing story whilst in a meeting with the directors and general manager of the company. The general manager, Bill, reminded the managing director of his statement at the commencement of the assignment.

Bill, I have put on a sales development company to boost the sales and formalise everything. Don't worry about what they are doing as it will not affect you at all.

Probably about a couple of weeks after our arrival on site, Bill had experienced the impact of revolution occurring on the front end of the business. He spent the next five months working with everyone, calming flustered feathers, acting as an advocate to the developer and reports that he spent at least half his week counselling people and situations. He was the counsellor and naturally took the role to keep the business moving to the desired goal.

He had no objection to the situation as the business achieved massive growth beyond anyone's expectations, but it certainly is an on-going point of humour to the senior management of the company. Maybe he has honed a new skill for himself for the future.

The managing director just smiled.

Chapter 12:

The Initial Barriers to Overcome in Becoming a Sales Focused Organisation

Amongst the many issues involved in taking a company from being product or financially based to being a sales focused company, are the matters that you will need to address directly with the sales team. Your understanding of some of the barriers you will encounter can greatly assist you in your preparation for success in the role of sales manager and in achieving a sales focused team.

One of the first issues you will be up against in any company is its existing culture, and, more importantly, that of its sales force and related personnel. This culture is, like any that has been in place in any company, quite entrenched and will resist your efforts to bring in change in order to preserve its values and status quo. You will need to pinpoint what you are facing to ensure you can manage through the series of situations you will inevitably face. Many managers fail in the first few weeks and months because they do not identify problems with enough clarity and are then not able to deal with them when they arise.

In most situations, a new sales manager or revolutionist will be contracted to take over the role of the previous sales manager. The previous manager will have left the company because of any number of reasons. These might well include deficient performance or the inability to manage the team (sometimes due to complacency, or even impending retirement). Very rarely is a sales manager moved into managing a new team for the purpose of recruiting or taking over an existing high performance team.

You may also be moving into a situation where the director of the company has been directly responsible for the day-to-day activities of the sales team. Some companies are evolving their businesses and eventually the directors get to the point where they wish to step back from this day-to-day involvement and concentrate on more strategic areas of the business.

How you approach these barriers is important. You need to consider carefully what you are dealing with in each individual situation and with each person. In some companies you might find not just one complex situation, but several, or various combinations of circumstances.

What is a new sales manager likely to encounter when taking over from a long term complacency situation?

- You will find that there is a strong loyalty to the predecessor, as the team were comfortable with the relaxed style of the complacent or disengaged person. These teams have been allowed to operate with little accountability and have gone about their business with the attitude that 'everyone just knows what they have to do'. In this instance, the philosophy of "near enough is good enough" reigns and no pressure is brought to bear on the team, with no reporting process to identify non-performance.

- The sales team have been educated into a certain method of operation and are usually blind (and resistant) to other methods or practices. The longer the team has been stable in such a situation, with limited 'new blood' being brought into the team or management, the more likely they will be to have closed opinions on how to go about operating.

- You are likely to find a dangerously high level of product/service loyalty, to the point, even, of really being one-eyed. At this stage, the culture can actually enter a phase referred to as 'self-sell', where they continually reinforce to everyone around them how wonderful their product or service is. Even in the face of diminishing sales results, the likely reaction is not to confront their problems but to increase the degree to which they are one-eyed, becoming even firmer in their conviction that the outside world is wrong and they, of course, are right.

- The sales team can be up to five to eight years behind market trends. This is because a lack of new ideas coming into the business results in the exhaustion of the ideas that worked some five to eight years ago. These ideas were successful at that time, and engendered an environment that promoted a complacency that has survived.

- The sales team have a very dogmatic approach to change. These teams are not used to change and do not know how to deal with it. There is considerable fear on their part, as dealing with change is a skill they have not yet acquired.

- If they are long-term employees, you will find the sales team may have inflated - and somewhat fragile - egos. Long-term employees will have often been over-rewarded by their management and become quite good friends with their fellow team members. In some cases, the team, and, indeed, the company, are like a second family. So, with egos that have been fuelled over a number of years by people towards whom they have very warm feelings, these people find it hard to accept a form of interaction other than that to which they are accustomed. And that status quo amounts to an ongoing reinforcement of their feelings about themselves.

- Objection to being measured and held accountable. These teams are convinced they are doing the best they possibly can and that there is no need for them to provide information or become involved in reporting functions so that they can be measured or, as a result, be made accountable. They actually do not want to know that they could have done something differently. Consistent with the points above, such as ego and complacency, this situation is a form of denial.

- Senior management constantly seek the team's opinions as they are unsure of their decision to employ and are influenced by the team's comments. This is a form of fear on the management's part. They have relationships with the team members and it can take them some time to deal with the shock of a new manager. They are quite nervous of losing other relationships within the company and require reinforcement that they have made the right decision. This is the most dangerous practice of all as it gives the team an option to 'remove' the new manager.

Seeking out the verification

We have often encountered situations where companies have embarked on the sales development process and fallen into one of the easiest problems. Prior to commencing down their chosen path, they have identified problems with the current sales force and consider they are not contributing what they are requiring in revenue and method of operation.

In some cases they have experienced sellers on the team who are running their own little business within the company. They do not share information nor do they assist the company in becoming smarter with their selling function.

Once the process is underway, the decision-makers will start to feel the change process and will be gathering different view points from everyone; as they arrive in their office to complain or give an opinion. Most managers are wary of this occurring and keep to a neutral ground so as not to undermine the change process.

However, managers who are unsure of their decision or are weak decision-makers, will seek the opinion of people in the company to reinforce their own standing. They need assurance that they have made the right decisions as they move into some unknown areas. Commonly the person they will ask is the person who has been employed in the sales force the longest. Rarely is that person enjoying the change and is the most affected by anything occurring so positive reinforcement is most unlikely. They would be considering leaving their role if the change persists.

Delivered on a platter

The moment a decision maker seeks the opinion of the sales force, particularly the more long term people, you have delivered on a platter the reason for the change process to fail. They are hearing exactly what they need to hear, your uncertainty in your decision and the chance to overthrow the situation. It is not their intent at the time but when such an opportunity presents itself, they cannot resist.

It takes only one moment's nervousness on the part of the decision-makers and the time and effort goes by the wayside.

If these situations sound serious and difficult, it is because they are. If you find you are walking into one or more of these situations, you must realise it will take tremendous strength and a dedicated focus on your part to bring the company through to where it needs to be.

Visualise yourself trying to move forward, and being followed by a giant magnet that is trying to pull you back all the time. The outcome boils down to

(a) who has the strongest pull, the new manager or the team, and

(b) the dedication of senior management and the directors to reinforcing and supporting your position in the company.

If either the new manager or the senior management/directors show a weakness, the company will not change

The Industry Legend

Many executives will be able to relate to this situation. While reviewing the sales performance of a family owned company, and while interviewing its team members, we were faced with a situation in which the issue of long term employees emerged as a key factor.

The company had been established for some 50 years and was quite successful. Its sales team members had been employed for an average of fifteen years each and one had been employed there all his working life.

The managing director, Ben, of the company was forward thinking and believed more market share was available to them. The company's market analysis provided ample evidence that this belief was justified. Ben came to us to assist him in getting that market share. However, on reviewing the sales team members, we were confronted with a person, George, who had been with the company many years and did not endorse our involvement. George espoused the view that their industry was vastly different from all others, and, therefore, sales in that industry could only be comprehended and handled by long-time professionals in that particular field. He further stated that no one without industry knowledge could possibly understand the hardships and stresses that a salesperson in that field undergoes to be successful. Only an experienced person could appreciate the high degree of product knowledge required and the level of service to each individual needed to sustain the business, not to mention the overall complexity of the business. George was adamant that this was like no other business; it was unique, and outsiders needed to appreciate and accept that.

We asked George why there was a difference between his sales results and those of two other sales people. His response was that his customers were far more demanding and he was basically always on call to them. He was obliged to cater to them completely, running to meet their every need, instantly, if he wanted them to continue as clients of the company.

After listening to his presentation on his performance, we asked George how long he had been in the industry. His reply was "Thirty years". We then asked him what other industries he had been employed in, either permanently or as a contractor. He replied "None".

Our next question to him was what form of measurement was he using to validate his statements in his presentation to us, if he had no real experience in other industries? How would he view his experience against, say, that of the one hundred industries our consultant had been involved with? Which had more validity and benchmarking worth?

We are still waiting for his answers.

The alternative situation you will be involved in is where you take over from a short-term manager. You will encounter:

- The sales team are strongly united and consider their abilities to be higher than that of the manager. As the team are potentially experienced at debunkering new managers, they have developed a view that as they have outlasted the managers their knowledge pool must be considerably higher. They do not consider the manager has left due to the lack of ability of the team/company to address change requirements or unworkable conditions within the company. The team members will not share information with the new manager.

- If they are non-performers they have learnt the skill to 'remove managers'. You will see this particularly in larger organisations where they have learnt to sit through the changes. They are aware what the senior management expect of the new sales managers and they work to ensure they contribute those factors to their results. The sales manager is always first to go over the sales team from a senior manager's perspective.

- The team is transient reflective of the previous manager/s. In some businesses the sales team can be quite transient. You will find this in call centres, commissions only teams and similar. There are no real systems and structure as no one is there long enough to implement or remember what has been done.

- Fluctuating levels of accountability. Sales Teams learn quickly that a new manager will usually start off with the approach 'a new broom sweeps well' and within a few short months have dropped most of the ideas that were started.

- Low motivation and work on the basis of 'sitting out the trend'. Again this is rampant in large organisations where they witness managers come and go in various sections of the business. If you sit there long enough - it will go away.

- Lack of culture and method in consistently achieving results. Due to the changes occurring at the top, the emphasis of why they are employed is lost in the day to day. The culture may have become, 'wait until the new manager gets here and we can make a decision then'. These teams are usually procrastinators and developed a strong resource of reasons why something cannot occur in sales.

Lights Out ! ! !

In a major corporation we were privy to an example of 'removing managers' by a very experienced and stubborn sales team. The company had three previous sales managers who had lasted only six to twelve months each time after a long term sales manager had departed. The long term manager was of a particular unique style and had employed three gentlemen and all very similar in style. We named them the three amigos. You could not split them up and it was nearly looking like a cloning scenario.

On first meeting the three gentlemen in a public forum, they quickly commenced 'boss bashing' their newest manager and did not speak highly of the company and its practices. This was brought to a halt as quickly as possible due to the environment.

On speaking with the company management afterwards, we were informed that these three gentlemen were all only average sales performers and they were experiencing some problems with them. They were defiant of the company, systems and management however they were unable to remove them due to the human resource environment of the company.

The newest manager, Peter, was most frustrated by them and was unable to manage through. He had tried sitting out their games, he had tried different angles with them. He had provided them with coaching, new directions, new customers and every other idea he could think of. Basically they were winning the game by just sitting him out. They had reached stalemate.

In a sales meeting one day, frustration reached an all time high with Peter as these people failed to contribute and were just wasting everyone's time again. On the spur of the moment, Peter stood up walked to the door to leave and as he departed he switched off the lights and closed the door behind him leaving them sitting in the dark. Lights Out!

Who Won ? The Three Amigos or Peter?

The first 90-120 days in the role will define your success or failure in both situations. If you do not take the correct steps and communicate this with the team, you will define your outcome. This first bracket of time is the most stressful and critical in successful professional sales team management.

Chapter 13:

Directors and Managers who Sabotage the Company's Growth

The single biggest issue that you, as a director or sales manager will confront is that management may not be totally dedicated to change. This includes the highest levels of management, such as the CEO, the managing director and/or the senior management team. Yet their complete commitment to change is essential if the company is to endure - and survive - the process of change.

Complete dedication to the change is necessary and you must remain focused on the outcome at all times, rather than on how rough the journey has become. Nothing will be achieved without pain and turmoil and the sign of a great director and senior management team is their ability to manage through all phases of the process. If you are endeavouring to undergo a revolution, then you must remember the pain and turmoil you are experiencing is not as bad as the situation that you would experience if you did not.

Sabotage - why does it happen?
You must always remain alert to the fact that a director or senior manager may actually sabotage the change process the company is undergoing and thereby, the company's growth. The sabotage is subconscious; it is not something they recognise in themselves, so others have to be vigilant. Change engenders a certain degree of turmoil and the result can be an atmosphere of discord. Some people have a low tolerance for this kind of atmosphere, and instead of accepting that the solution is to move on with the change, to make the necessary improvements and create a better situation for all, they 'cross to the other side'. They start to think back to the past, overlooking the period of downturn that brought about the need for change, and start to talk about how good things used to be - before the turmoil or complaints. They start looking to others for answers, generally to those who instigated the revolution or change in the first place. Be wary - it takes only one person to splinter from the initial goals and then the process will fall apart.

If the managing director is the major financial stakeholder in the business, then the likelihood of change, and having the change go through smoothly, is much greater than where the business is managed by a board of directors who do not have financial investment in the business. The reason for this is accountability. The director with a major investment has final accountability and will make the tough decisions required to keep the business moving. In companies where the board is managing (whether directly or indirectly), then the level of accountability is reduced as most decisions are made by consensus. As noted in earlier chapters, quite often the change process is reprioritised.

The change process through revolution requires strong decision-makers at the top. It is a difficult process, but the results usually outweigh the pain of the journey.

You will never forget week six

The most likely time for things to fall apart is week six. Week six is somewhat like doomsday in change management when doing revolutions. This is when the old habits are being broken and a lot of change is going on; people are stretched to the limit and employees are pulling hard for the good old days. SFI has surveyed, experienced and documented many instances demonstrating that week six is the deciding period in the change process, the time in which the success or failure of the project is determined.

At this stage of the change process, personnel will start working very hard on the management, stressing the negatives of the change (never the positives), pointing out how it will damage the business, and finding ways to justify how it is impossible for this to work. They put forward the view that because 'they are out there in the market, talking to the customers', they are in a position to know all the answers. (That's why the business is in the shape it's in.) They use the full extent of their selling skills on their own management to regain control of the situation.

Other areas of the company that are also being affected by change, will also start pulling the company in different directions, all intent in finding the security of how things were. If you are not a strong decision-maker and stay dedicated to your decision then you can permanently damage the business. There are many companies that suffer from failure and the inability to succeed with any change work as the employees have learnt to bunker down and outlast management.

There are many reasons why everything seems to reach a head at the six week mark (sometimes it's seven or five but we can assure people they will experience it). We often use the metaphor that it is like a rubber band being stretched to its full capacity at this point. The longer the stretching is held, the more likely the rubber band will lose its strength and take on a new shape.

Companies are not really all that different than this metaphor.

As with all change processes, this sales development and revolution process reaches into the other areas of the business and the elements of accountability that it introduces often makes many of the other line managers quite nervous, as they feel they may be exposed. In some cases, these people take personal offence at the fact that something they worked hard to create is being done away with or changed. Their feeling is that their project or area is being sidelined and they often feel slighted, especially when the change process establishes that their way of doing things is flawed.

Your strength, tactic and dedication will define the outcome of your revolution.

Change and the management
The change process is difficult for everyone, but it is most difficult for the management. The need for counselling (by independent individuals) should never be underestimated. Managers need to be able to air their thoughts and reactions in a situation where they feel the person they are speaking to is objective and has no allegiances within the company.

Why is change so hard for management?

There are a number of factors that contribute to this being the case. When a company director or senior management team establishes a business, the process they go through is similar to what people go through when they set up a home. Much thought and many dreams go into the ideal company, the people, the wins and what benefits it will achieve. They envisage - and bring to reality - what the company will look like; its business image and the premises. They think about and decide where the company will be located, how its office will be decorated and furnished, and they think about their product or service.

These ingredients make up the company, and, as a business unfolds, in the owner's mind, their dream is being fulfilled. We often see people who live for a dream and who are dedicated to achieving it. Whether it will be worthwhile when they get there is not the deciding factor. It is a dream, an aspiration and to achieve this provides them with the reward of being there.

People who put their heart and soul into building their businesses are understandably very emotional about them. This results in people being very reluctant to undergo change. It is common knowledge, for example, that family owned companies are the least likely to change even in the face of adversity.

As the mantel collects dust
When you ask a company director to change the business, we often use the allegory of the mantelpiece as a device to explain the process and the reaction people often have to change.

People use their mantelpieces to display valued possessions. Each item is strategically placed on the mantel to display it for the world to see. Many mantels remain undisturbed, with the items displayed on them unchanged for many years.

Imagine a typical mantel: Let's say the mantel decoration consists of a vase at each end, a clock in the centre, two family photos and two pieces of holiday memorabilia. Your favourite oil painting hangs proudly over the whole arrangement.

One day, during a cleaning spree, your partner decides to change things around. One vase is removed and placed on a side table. A new item from another room is put in its place. The painting is replaced with another family favourite, and the two photos are split up and placed at either end of the mantel. The clock stays in the middle and the trip memorabilia remains.

You are presented with the change and initially, you think, "This is a nice change, it looks fresh and balances with the room." About two weeks down the track you shift the photos back together. After another few weeks, the second vase reappears, and the new item that took its place is shifted along a little.

After a couple of months the vase replacement is removed and then the old painting comes back to its place of pride over the fireplace.

The thought of change was very promising, but now you just want things back where they were comfortable

If this were a business where you had spent many hours making changes, you will now be at loggerheads with the company directors. You have proven logically that the new system works, the team is winning, and the results are coming in. The director has let go of the reins (many are inclined to be involved spasmodically with the sales area).

Then the director may start to discuss the changes with others and unconsciously refer to past times. They may even seek the staff's opinion on how it's all going. All these instances can be harmless chats - or they can signal serious problems ahead for the change.

We have reviewed many organisations where change was attempted. In each case, the directors cited many reasons explaining why it was not successful. These directors had given their approval for the change, but were personally unable to accept the business operating in a different direction. They were uncomfortable and uneasy with the process and sabotaged it so that it ended before it could be completed. This permitted them to state that the process hadn't worked at all, and to justify stopping it.

Don't judge a book by its cover - unless you're in marketing

The following was experienced first hand by SFI in an Australian company involved in the national retail distribution of its products. This company was one of the first to establish their product line in the country and enjoyed several years of strong trading, building its turnover to approximately $5 million per annum.

A family-run enterprise, the company had a few local investors to assist in its growth requirements. Lee, the managing director, was responsible for the general management of the business, including sales and marketing. He had little commercial business experience, no real sales and marketing experience. His past experience was with another small local family company, located in a rural town.

Lee made the decision that would define the outcome of the business. He was completely confident that his decision was best, and his loyal staff supported this decision absolutely.

SFI elected to leave the business, convinced that this group of people lacked the ability to follow through on what was required.

In hindsight, Lee undoubtedly regrets his decision. In the course of time, the other directors moved a vote of no confidence and had him removed to a passive role in the production area. The stores did not accept the company's attempt at a second approach - they had already been burnt because the company had not provided the changes as required. The company's good sales personnel left, and only those people who felt loyal to the firm remained. The competitors moved in, and all that was left for the company's product was low-grade shelf space, guaranteeing low stock turnover. Revenue became now average; profits were low when there were any at all.

The company could have easily doubled its sales - if only they had been able to operate commercially instead of emotionally. What Lee did was subconscious sabotage of the business.

We have since found out that this business was sold with an enormous trading debt. Lee remained with the company and now works at a lowly paid, unskilled position with no responsibility.

The agenda person
With the managing director and senior team on board, the next hurdle you have to overcome is the 'agenda person'. These people exist in sales, and you certainly have them in sales development.

Always remember that there are people in senior management who agree to the change process primarily because they see it as an opportunity to jockey for position.

There are occasionally other reasons, but whatever they might be, it is wise to be aware of the agenda person.

Most of the problems surrounding the change process are the result of uncertainty on the part of directors or other senior management. There

was a fundamental lack of commitment to the decision and/or a lack of thought before making a decision. If these people question the decision to undergo the process of change, and cannot be persuaded to fully support the
process, then there is little hope for a successful change. This may be the result of a lack of due diligence in making the decision or in an inability to cope with change at either management or company level. It can also mean a fundamental lack of confidence in the company to actually achieve results in the market place.

As cited in the chapter on companies that achieve change, very few companies actually have the ability and strength to achieve the change, and very few can admit they are not capable of coping with change.

It is essential that all companies that recognise the need for change recognise also that people can become intimidated or upset by the process, both at management and staff level. Any management implementing change must prepare itself with all the safeguards possible. Where management is fainthearted, change will never work.

Chapter 14:

The Working Sales Plan

The soundness of your sales plan will define the soundness of your business. Business planning skills have developed and grown over the past decades to demand accuracy of financial budgets, market analysis, SWOT analysis, growth funding and the other incremental information required for the ongoing development of the company. Most companies have developed strong fiscal and inventory control measures. The main lack in all this, as always, is in sales, which remains in the 'grey', with measurement and plans based on fiscal requirements only.

A typical business plan in sales consists predominantly of product and finance based information. Generally, no validation of the business plan takes place, and it is merely the cumulative requirements of the business. The final figure usually is 'the amount of money we need in the coming year'.

The 'how' factor
The reason most businesses fail to meet or exceed their budgets is that they lack the 'how' factor. And what is the 'how' factor? It's simple - it's how much effort it takes to actually get the sales. This is the validation of everything.

Generally, a business plan that is written for a new business is based on hypothetical situations and estimates of the business performances. Very few businesses are actually built by duplicating another, and with enough information and experience to validate what is required. In other words, very few people avail themselves of existing examples to set themselves up in business. As a rule, businesses evolve in what may be viewed as a natural or market driven manner.

For example, a business may evolve from a group of staff members deciding to leave the company where they learned about their particular industry to go out on their own, or a business may be the result of a well-sold investment opportunity. Another way a business often starts is with a person who feels an affiliation with a particular product or service.

However it is that a business evolves, if they bother with a plan at all, the result is usually hypothetical, based on estimates or minimum requirements for sustaining itself in the market.

How does a plan actually help?

How often do you hear of a person going out and selling a concept to test the market to know the actual level of effort involved and then setting up a business? This is rare indeed, even though it is quite obvious that this sort of forethought would save companies millions if they took that approach. No doubt, there is some correlation between this lack of testing and why many new business start-ups fail in their first couple of years. Market research for product suitability is fine, but you still need to test 'how much effort and over what period of time does it take to get the sales results to validate your plan'.

When an existing business writes a plan, it tends to be based on last year's performances, economic growth, new markets being entered and other contributing factors. Yet these plans are also hypothetical, as no process of rationalisation or validation of achievability is entered into. It may be a different approach, but it still involved working over the same
old philosophy.

We mentioned earlier in the book that in a review of one hundred sales budgets, we found that 97% could be achieved in two thirds of the working week. Therefore, if you assume that any of these companies could easily either increase its effort or increase its performance, it would be reasonable to expect that companies could achieve greater returns. This sort of knowledge is developed through correct sales planning, which finalises the budget.

The purpose of the sales plan is to provide a road map to making money for the company

It follows, therefore, that the clearer the road map, the more positive the result. This road map must include all the details of exactly how much effort is required of the sales force, in which directions they will expect to be going, what quality of performance will be expected of them and which customer groups to target. In showing a company the exact road to travel, a sales plan will result in sales that exceed their fiscal requirements.

Your role as a sales manager is to write the plan and then to manage, coach and guide the team according to what you've written.

What about the wrong plan?

There is danger if an inexperienced manager writes the plan, or if an experienced manager writes the wrong plan, the risk of failure is considerably higher than if a company just lurches out into the market place without any advance planning and conducts its business in a reactive manner. Therefore, the plan must be reviewed for its soundness, and benchmarks identified and agreed upon to ensure its accuracy and viability.

Unfortunately many business plans do fail as managers skip these last essential steps, which are what makes them move from the realm of the theoretical to the real.

Never forget that as a sales manager, you will be measured by the performance of the team. If you take the time write the right plan, you will ensure your position as well as recognition for being a quality manager who produces results.

Chapter 15:

Reporting Systems

The necessary evil

The function of reporting has been a source of frustration to management since time began. It is a particularly frustrating exercise to extract reports from sales teams and ensuring the accuracy of these reports is another major problem. Most reports are stand-alone and provide specific information to specific divisions within the company. Very rarely do they inter-relate to assist the sales team in becoming stronger. As sales people usually operate on a fairly flexible timetable, and in many cases, away from the office, the reporting function becomes more important and, increasingly, a greater point of contention in a company.

The quality of reports from person to person can vary and the timelines in which they are presented is also a cause of frustration. Managers are often faced with the problem of having to continually chase the reports, wasting enormous amounts of their time. And the moment they take the focus away from the report or let staff know that it can be late, the natural reaction of the sales staff is that they slacken off even more on producing the paperwork.

Over the years a great variety of reports has been created and time involvement can vary from company to company. Depending on what is expected in any given company, some reports are completed in one hour and in some cases, they can take some five to six hours out of the staff member's week.

What reports are actually productive?

The purpose of the reporting systems in the sales area of a business is to measure performance and outcomes against the sales plan. Therefore it is important to ensure that if you are asking sales people to complete paperwork or reporting systems then you must:

    1. ensure they are in line with the sales plan,

2. provide them with feedback so that they can improve their performance, and

3. they provide business intelligence to support decision making,

The consistent use of 'reports and feedback' to the team will assist in bringing consistent results to the company.

It would be a very poor manager who insists on reports from their team but doesn't provide immediate weekly feedback on performance based issues

Under traditional management styles, sales people were asked to complete a 'run or route sheet'. This outlined what customers they called on, some basics of what occurred during the appointment, and their personal perspective of the customer situation and viability for the next order. There may also have been a tick box section on products.

Many sales people have joked that they have written derogatory comments about the managers and/or company into these reports and that these remarks have gone unnoticed. Many of you reading this book remember hearing of this - or may have done this themselves - at some stage of their selling career.

What is the purpose of reports of this kind?
You are taking up valuable selling time having reports of this kind filled in. If you examine their format, you will see that these reports have a fundamental flaw: the information requested does not directly measure against a performance; it is subjective and therefore not relevant. The information on the customer is not stored in a central access location, so it is not relevant, as it cannot be used. Information that cannot be accessed and therefore used may as well not exist at all. Furthermore, most of the information requested and provided in this type of report consists of personal opinion only, so, again, it isn't relevant.

You can actually achieve the same information from a financial report of customer performance and sales to date/gross margins which most financial departments can produce on a daily basis, so why request a report at all?

Why do you require reports?

Financial reports and route reports do not address the information you need to professionally lead and coach a group of sales people. It will give you some disjointed information but you will not really be able to assist the team. They will not understand what impact on the company or their individual results this information represents. What you are doing is preventing everything from being congruent and measurable, which, in effect, means keeping everything in the grey.

A sales force really needs only five reports, whether it consists of internal or external sales personnel.

They are:

- *Performance development systems*

- *Customer information records (CRM)*

- *Knowledge base (which differs from a CRM)*

- *Financial reports*

- *Pipeline reports*

These are five reports critical to the productive and pro-active management of sales personnel, using these against the sales plan will guarantee your success. They all interlink and validate each other to ensure you are working with facts and not stories. They require a focused manager to work with them, one that is genuinely desiring to increase the performance of the sales people and revenue of the company.

The manager then must have in place business intelligence that is going to provide more forensic information. This enables them to establish accurate forecasts, minimise leakage of lost opportunities and sales. Moreover it will assist them in being able to operate the business to achieve growth.

We do warn managers however that those using 'probability factors' on pipeline reports or sales reports are at the highest risk. This is a dated reporting methodology and is the common thread that we find in all companies we work with or whom attend our seminars that are experiencing lack of growth or financial problems.

We often say 'if you are using probability factors then you are probably going broke!' Heed the warning and work with facts rather than subjective information. The performance development system will give you utmost clarity of whether a sale is likely to come as its behavioural based information.

The business intelligence combined with the other reporting indicated will give you the most accurate facts to work with and provide you with the information you need to drive the business forward.

Chapter 16:

Job Descriptions and Contracts

Once you have your sales plan in place, there are certain activities that flow on from it. It is at this stage that you can start to tie the ingredients of the plan together.

The job description and contract are developed based on the content of the sales plan, and you must make certain each element is complete to ensure the overall objectives of the company are met. The job description will also form part of your recruitment plan and job specifications. The more you ensure that all the elements are linked, the more sound the basis upon which the plan is implemented.

The job description - how does it help?
For many years, those companies that had any job descriptions in writing at all relied on a series of soft statements outlining the general scope of a role. We find that many people have job descriptions in place to satisfy various requirements, usually issues arising out of their human resource areas. They don't, as a rule, see them as the valuable tool that they can be, ultimately contributing to the company's success.

What, then, are the essential components of a useful job description? The job description is a vital document that outlines exactly what the role of the sales person is, as well as what quality and quantity of performance you require of them.

The more clarity in the job description - the better the result that the person will contribute

The key is to ensure there is specific and direct instruction within the document.

That the job description is a document with some weight must be conveyed to the employee. You are seeking commitment from the sales people on signing, not just asking them to complete a paperwork function.

The employment contract

Another essential component of the sales plan. Just as with the job description, the contract is another important document and not just some piece of bureaucracy an employee must wade through to get the job. When you enter into a contractual agreement with new employees, you are asking them to take on a commitment.

Laws governing these arrangements will vary from country to country, and state to state, but commitment is what you are seeking no matter where the person is located and what local law and custom dictate.

A good contract will include the minimum requirements you expect of the performance of the role, using such criteria as the number of appointments, the minimum sales values and other specifics that you can apply to the particular position. It will also identify all the reporting requirements you have of the employee and specify what means you will be using to measure the qualitative and quantitative factors of their employment.

Failure to comply with these requirements is a basis for termination, and this, also, must be spelled out in the contract. The sales person who signs this style of contract is signalling their confidence in their abilities and the results will follow. Those who are reluctant to sign, you will find, are not committed to the role nor are they confident of the outcome.

Conversely, managers who are unwilling to use contracts of this nature are signalling their own reluctance to confront these very tough issues.

Do not be put off by the prospect of producing a very long document. It is vital to include all details of the position and the expectations you have of it, ensuring there are no grey areas and that the prospective employee knows exactly where they stand. This is the document an employee will be signing, and there should be no areas with a question mark over them. Ensure you use plain English - there is no need to resort to obscure and confusing language. Don't forget - this is an exercise in clarity, not mystification.

The job description must be a working document against which you measure performance regularly. Do not let it become a piece of paper that is lost after the person starts with your organisation.

This is the contract of agreement between you and your sales team members. They should be aware that you are measuring their performance against this document at all times. It is also useful to use in designated performance reviews.

This is the foundation of your recruitment plan/specifications and will define the quality of person you are going to employ or what education is needed for existing personnel.

The job description must describe exactly what you need to be successful and each time you sacrifice or replace one of the skills you will sacrifice your chances of success.

This document will also tie over to career pathing. It will assist people within the company to understand what skills they need to develop in order to move up the ladder within your company.

Chapter 17:

Salary

The next question is always money.

If you review what you have done in the past and what you need in the future, there are a number of elements to consider from the salary package on offer. In the past, companies have offered relatively stable or fixed salary packages to attract a stable style of operator. The implementation of incentives has been miniscule, particularly in product based environments. Companies are concerned about the ramifications packages that vary from the mainstream might have for other areas of the business.

Before deciding what you are going to offer in the package, consider what type of person you want to attract.

- Do you want someone who is opportunity focused?

- Do you want someone who doesn't have a problem asking for money or for the order?

- Do you want a person who can work a situation and produce results for the company?

- Does the salary package on offer by the company, actually attract the style of operator you are seeking?

The method in which you pay your personnel will also define what the outcome will be. An interesting finding in the sales research report is what sales people actually respond to in salaries.

Money makes the world go 'round'
People have always believed that sales people respond to money. In fact, this is not so. Research shows that only 16% of sales people claim they are motivated by money, and, in effect, only 8% were actually genuinely motivated by money. This attitude predominates in product-based environments.

Sales people are, in the main, motivated by security and reward for achievement through recognition or material items/events that can be shared with their families and partners. These mainstream sellers are very systematic in their approach to selling, they are a little shy on the closing or about asking for money, and may not identify opportunities that are before them. They certainly do not usually actively open opportunities, as they are in the main reactive sellers.

When hiring, look at the results your applicants are producing. Is their style what you want for your company? Do you want your sellers to identify opportunities, do you want them to be good at closing, or does the sales person have little overall impact on the results of the company? In other words, are you hiring for a company who has such a strong reputation in the market place that it has a high level of momentum - such as companies like Coca-Cola?

If you want a flat salary person, then the good news for companies is that this can be very cost effective against the cost of sales where they are not just seeking commission components.

If you want a commission component salary package person, then you have to carefully evaluate what level of commission and what structure you have in place to ensure you benefit the company and the sales person. The way you structure the salary package will define the performance of the people.

SFI does not recommend the 'one size fits all' approach for sales people. Although easier to administer, you have to consider what sales people are employed to do. Sell and look for more selling opportunities. If you are paying a flat salary, you are attracting a person who is seeking maintenance and security. They will therefore want to look for that maintenance and security by calling on existing customers.

Getting the Right Person
The company was a small business with a good product. They had established a commission structure that was based on half salary and half commission. The base salaries were quite high and the average person could lead a very nice lifestyle on that base level.

On reviewing the performances of two sales people, Peter and John, it was found that both were under-performing, at a level of less than 20% of budget.

During private counselling Peter said that he was driven by money but it came through that he needed assistance in how to actually work through sales opportunities. With that assistance applied, there was an immediate upturn and focus in his behaviour.
John, however, responded to a private counselling session with the news that he was seeking a position elsewhere. He did not consider it necessary to work any harder than he was currently and in his view, the problem was that the products didn't fit the market and not his selling.

John decided to leave his job and handed his leads to Peter. On telephoning one lead that John described as 'no opportunity', Peter questioned the potential customer and found an enormous on-going opportunity behind the initial sale. The customer required a customised approach (not too far from the company offerings) and good business was secured. So, who would you want to employ, Peter or John? The commission on offer is obviously not enough to guarantee results, and it basically comes back to your recruiting abilities.

The salary package is only a component and not the 'be all and end all' for great performers. The environment and structure they work in are the key to your success. The package helps, but your ability to lead, coach and guide will be a major contributor. There is not a ready supply of great sellers in the market place, nor is there a ready supply of managers who can make an average seller great through coaching, guidance and structure.

Consider what you are applying around the salary package when considering the package. If the company has no back end structure to deliver, then you won't want to employ someone with a high commission component. The higher the component, the more pressure they can apply to the business. The highest level of commission is full commission: they are there for the money in most cases. People on these packages will traditionally rarely show concern for the customer or the back end of the business.

This is not say you should avoid this kind of arrangement if you think it can work for you, but if you do go this way, ensure that the back end is prepared for front end pressure.

Choose the package carefully and choose the seller even more carefully

CHAPTER 18:

Career Pathing

Career pathing is a stage that is often overlooked by companies, generally because they don't understand its function or requirements. This is more prevalent in smaller companies who are focused on survival rather than growth.

Career pathing has two significant purposes: to assist new or existing employees understand what future is provided at the company and the skill bases they need; and so that a company can meet the needs of its current and potential client base.

A company's current and future customer base
The primary driver in the development of a career path is the company's current customer base and its potential future customer base. You have to decide what kind of customer service personnel you require to meet the needs of your customers. Is the business largely made up of high volume accounts across a number of territories with only limited key account selling requirements? Is the company made up of a series of sales teams across various states? Perhaps it reaches into a high level of selling across a number of verticals or categories, or maybe it's a high call centre environment.

With the customer base in mind, the sales manager must develop a method of meeting their needs in both servicing and the personnel's skill. Consider what level of service the customer may receive from competitors - and make sure your company betters it. Further, the sales manager should be able to identify several levels of selling within the company. This is not as difficult as it might sound, as there would be very few (perhaps only a handful) companies in this world that can manage with a 'one size fits all' approach to selling.

How does this help the company?
From the sales plan you will be able to identify the people required and the skill levels of each of those people. Job descriptions will be written for all roles nominating exactly what skills, experience and other details are

needed as outlined in the chapter on Job Descriptions. These become fixed documents of the company, allowing employees and potential employees to understand what is required to progress in the company.

No one wants to work in a dead-end job. Most employees want to know that there is scope to grow, develop and take on more responsibility in their positions. They want to further their career options and quality of knowledge. If you have people currently working for you who do not see this as a basic requirement, you have a recruitment problem, and more than likely a return on investment issue.

Employees evaluate companies on what they can do for them, while employers are assessing what the potential employee can do for them. A career path is going to achieve two major results. The first is that it will attract people who are more motivated and driven to develop themselves while the company benefits from their energy. And the second is that this compels the company to adhere to a strict recruitment policy rather than just hiring on gut feel and regretting the decision the next day.

What's in a name?
Giving titles to positions is another issue that faces management. Sales people want to be called everything but sales people - even though they've chosen sales as their career.

Names of a sales role can be any combination of the following:

> Sales Representative, Sales Engineer, Sales Consultant, Account Executive, Territory Representative, Business Development Consultant, Product Specialist, Customer Representatives, Service Representative - and the list goes on.

The next group consists of the next level up and these could be:

> Territory Manager, Sales Manager, Key Account Executive, Key Account Manager, Business Development Manager, Product Manager, State Sales Manager, National Sales Manager, Customer Service Manager, Team Leader, etc.

These lists have the potential to go on indefinitely.

An important consideration and one that is most often overlooked when handling titles out is the customer's point of view. Are they liable to recognise what role the person has from the title? Do they have any idea who they're agreeing to meet with? Be sure your titles make sense.

A rose by any other name

Peter worked for a manufacturing company as sales manager. This company's products were not of a particularly high value in engineering terms, but provided a volume sales 'easy buy' product for clients and their customers. It was a well-used product, but the company was really doing no more than shifting numbers. The duties of the positions in the company became repetitive and it was hard to attract candidates who were prepared to stay on for more than twelve months.

Peter was recruiting for new personnel and had developed a series of career growth options for the employees. He was determined to build more value into the roles from an employee's perspective with the view to retaining them longer.

On advertising for a sales representative, he decided to call the position 'Sales Manager for a product division'. The concept worked and the telephones rang and resumes arrived in quantities never before seen. He had packaged the salary nicely to cover growth in the territory, and included a good base retainer.

Peter ended up employing Roger, who was interested in the title and was prepared to work for the salary package being offered. Roger's skill base was not as strong as that of his predecessor, but he did have many qualities and he had a good grasp of fundamental selling techniques. He was also a very likeable person.

After a few months on the road, Roger was having a discussion with Peter about why sales for a particular account were dropping. The company in question had always been a loyal and major customer for the past sales representative, but now their business just seemed to be falling away. Roger had discussed various options with the customer, but to no avail. He asked Peter to visit to find out what the problem was.

Peter visited the customer, who was most surprised to see him. He said he thought Peter had moved on and that Roger was the new sales manager. The customer went on to say how he had been surprised at the company's decision to employ a new sales manager with such obviously limited experience.

His view was that the company must be experiencing problems if it was downgrading the level of their management. He told Peter that the new manager did not seem to understand the issues in his business. He was gradually transferring his loyalties to a competitor.

The lesson here is that the titles you give your staff have meaning. If you call a person a manager, then customers will think that person is a manager, and has the skills, experience and responsibility that a manager usually has. Handing out management titles is not always a good thing. And employees who only work for titles may not be the ones you want or need.

A formal approach to career pathing is a step that can take the grey out of management and turn it into a black and white situation that everyone can work with and, most importantly, understand.

Good sales people look for a career path. They want to know that they too can climb the corporate ladder, and have a shot at a leadership role. Given the nature of the profession, these people in particular are very drawn to the security of a management role, as quickly as possible. And, like anyone else, they are also drawn to the status of the title 'Manager'.

Very few people wish to remain sales representatives all their working lives. Management should remain sensitive to the fact that there are only so many months or years that most people can operate consistently on the road and in the role. There are some people however that really do enjoy the lifestyle. Similarly, a customer service person or telemarketer can only operate so many months (not often years) on the telephones. They all strive for titles that are perceived as better and for the status that comes with such positions as national sales manager or national call centre manager for an organisation.

What motivates these people? Some are unable to tolerate the social stigma that is often part of being a sales person and others are high-energy people who want to make it to the top.

Many companies fall foul of their employees during times of promotion because sales people, just like anyone else, find it hard to understand or respect a decision giving someone any higher position over them. Employees will usually have a more intimate knowledge of how the promoted person operates, what work levels they actually do put in, and what short-cuts they may be taking as sales people. Knowing that the opportunity for promotion was imminent, these people will probably have been trying to position themselves to be in line for that higher position.

Sales people always seem to know before management when an employee is leaving and a position therefore coming up. By the time the appointment is made, they will have made up their minds that they were entitled to the position and when an associate is promoted over them, there is bound to be discontentment in the company. This can be the cause of cultural problems or can cause the amplification of existing cultural problems.

In instances where a person is seen to have been promoted well beyond their ability, some people leave within a few months as a result of the appointment. They lose respect for the management and the company, because they cannot understand the decision. Nor is it usually explained clearly to them why the position was filled with the chosen candidate. This scenario is particularly common in companies where vacancies are advertised internally before being put to the open market. SFI strongly recommends that all vacancies be advertised internally and externally simultaneously.

Career pathing is particularly important if you wish to attract a higher quality of team member. Knowing that your company offers structured Career pathing gives both the applicant and current employees confidence that the company takes a structured approach to their development, and that they will be able to easily identify what skills they need to hone in order to ensure they are positioning themselves to gain promotion.

CHAPTER 19:

Recruitment of Top Sellers and Managers

Companies are often bewildered by the sales people they employ, and wonder why it's all going so wrong. The people they hired started out looking like such good candidates, but nothing great ever seems to come of their work. Their results fluctuate and something just seems to be missing in their performance. Let's face it - they just don't set the world on fire.

Is this a familiar picture? If so, read on.

Confronted with such a situation, most companies look back and believe that it all started going awry after the first few months (at least, that's when they started noticing the problems). In fact, if they were to analyse the situation, they would realise that it all went wrong on the day they ran the advertisement, followed by when they conducted the interview. If things are going to go wrong with a sales person, you will find it commonly all stems back to your recruitment process.

Why the rush?
The recruitment process is the foundation for your results. Unfortunately, this process is often undertaken in haste or, in some cases, in sheer desperation to get a person on board. When a vacancy appears in the company, managers are under extreme pressure to find a replacement to maintain service levels to the customer base. Very few have an alternative plan to carry them over during the downtime that happens without the team member. Most managers are not even sufficiently in touch with the team to anticipate the problem.

The recruitment process is a very involved one and requires skills and due diligence to ensure the correct candidate is found. You will have the job description that has been developed based on the requirements of the company. This is the easy part. The hardest element of the whole procedure is the selection of the candidate to fit that company's requirements. If you don't recruit regularly, you will encounter many problems and pitfalls during the process.

If we consider how many jobs are advertised in the newspapers or over the Internet, then we will have a sense of where and how our companies fit in, and where the positions we advertise fit. Some companies bring strong branding to their job advertisements, some industries are 'trendy' and new vogue, others go for the prestige market, and then there are those that are fundamental to keeping the world going around.

Always remember that your personal excitement for the position is not always going to be an accurate predictor of the candidate's excitement for the role.

If you pick up the paper or go online and review the job sections, you will see a myriad of opportunities for people in a number of sales roles. All of these advertisements make promises of great incomes, lifestyle, career opportunities, travel and every other promise you would want to hear if you were looking for a new job.

Experienced sales people can generally read between the lines on most advertisements so the ones that are 'tricky' are not necessarily going to attract good candidates.

Imagine yourself looking for a new job. Are you going to be interested in the job with the 'leading software organisation' or the one in the ad that says 'we are a small family business'? If you are honest with yourself, the first advertisement will be your preference. It automatically prompts thoughts of a financially secure position, with easy recognition when selling the products, not to mention a range of good products and good systems within the company for use in the servicing of customers and so on.

The second advertisement gives rise to thoughts of a financially limited, small business, with little room for career development, the risk of potential supply problems, and the domination of family loyalty over all other issues and interests in the company. Another issue with family businesses is that most sales people believe they require a far higher level of accountability than larger organisations.

We do not wish to pigeonhole different kinds of companies here and say that they all fit into a particular stereotype, but in sales, a whole range of preconceived notions regarding the nature of companies, based on size and management, is linked with the marketplace.

How do I get the right person for my company?

What are you offering potential employees when you advertise the position in the market place? Can you rely on major name branding or the popularity of your industry? Are you working with the latest technology with which everyone wants to be involved? Is your product a high value seller with enormous opportunity and acceptance in the market place? If you can, then you are in the lucky ten percent of businesses.

If you belong in the other ninety percent, then you are in a business that is working hard to bring in the revenue, produce the results and keep the customers well serviced while holding your market share. What you are offering to the market place is probably long hours, hard work, high accountability, average salary - in other words, all those key words that send up red flags, preventing you from attracting quality candidates. In fact, at worst, you may only be attracting people who have been pushed out of other industries for any number of reasons and are desperate for a break.

As a sales manager you have to accept that some jobs are a 'hard slog' while other roles are relatively easy, and be able to identify which are which. As the manager you need to package both options so that they are appealing to the ideal candidate without over-dressing the situation, which can result in real disappointment on the part of the candidates and the company. This is a situation, which should establish your ability as a sales person: you must be able to package the position and ensure that it is, overall, an enjoyable job in a good working environment on a day-to-day basis. Where you find you're trying to promote a somewhat mundane job, you can offer good social activities, a positive working environment and rewards to offset the focus on the routine aspect of the role. This turns out to be a nicely packaged role that will work well for both the employee and employer.

What do I actually need?

Look closely at your business and, most importantly, your customer base. What do your customers want? If your business is built around regular account calls within a set geographical area, then you want a very steady and reliable person who is motivated by an institutional environment. You want someone who likes to work in a predictable environment with an emphasis on a high level of customer service and reliability. This person will do the best job of servicing your customers. Not only that, they are easier to manage as they are working from the institutional base and therefore quite predictable, with only minimal variations from one person to the next.

Breaking the Clone Process

In the SFI training and recruitment area, we have often encountered people who are clearly misfits; who were not employed to meet the company's requirements. A good example of this was a person who was employed in a long-established hospitality supply business.

The sales force was stable and the sales manager had been promoted from within, yet the company was losing market share and was battling to open new account opportunities. The existing sales people managed their territories in a very institutionalized manner. They did not have new business development skills and were therefore unable to adopt the behaviour needed to secure new business.

Things continued downward. On receiving resignations from two of their long-term employees, the management immediately recruited people who fitted the current company profile. As a management team they felt comfortable with the profile but failed to understand the company's need for sales people who had the right skill set for business development.

The company continued to suffer market loss and struggled to achieve new business development through their existing team. In brief, this really comes to an attitude problem and a definite skill problem on the part of the management.

If you have a young business that needs high-energy sales effort to move into a financially sound position, then you certainly don't want to recruit from a company such as the one in our little story. You need someone driven by new business selling and who wants to operate on the coalface. If your company wants a significant increase in sales, then that is the kind of sales person who can contribute to those goals - although one must remember that they are more difficult to manage. They can change from day to day, and are extremely demanding of their management.

When the misfit is the right fit

SFI was asked to recruit a sales person for a multinational software company. The position was to service existing accounts but primarily to develop new business. The salary package was geared to reward high achievers. A candidate emerged; Steve was a high-energy seller with a strong background in conceptual selling and sound closing skills in business-to-business environments. His personality was strong and he had a low tolerance for fools. What drove him was commission. On reviewing his application, the software company was unsure whether Steve would fit in with them. He was not the usual style of person they employed; in fact, he was significantly different from the rest of the team. After a number of conversations and meetings, they decided to 'give him a try'.

What was the result of this experiment?

In the first three months of employment, Steve achieved the highest figures of the entire company's Australian sales team - and this consisted of some forty people nationally. In the second quarter he achieved the single highest sale in the company's history, and was still over budget when this sale was deducted from his figures. In the final two quarters Steve had secured national and international sales levels that exceeded anyone's expectations.

At this point, the company didn't know what to do with him. He had sold well beyond the company's vision. Management were forced to rethink their business plan - very quickly.

Now, if you had to have a misfit, this one wasn't too bad, don't you think?

The lesson from this anecdote is that when you recruit, you must remember that it's about being able to identify the needs of the company and client base, rather than continuing to believe you must fit the existing culture. The existing culture may not be bringing in the results that are actually out there as a potential for your company.

As a recruiter you need to be able to work with your options just as marketers work with theirs. Adopt your buyer's perspective when you are recruiting, and make sure your candidates really meet the needs of your company.

It all starts at the top
If you wish to be a successful recruiter, then there is one fundamental fact you must accept: bad sales people are a sign of bad management. Invariably, you will find that sales people who don't do well are the product of poor and unthought-out recruitment methods, inferior management and confusing and conflicting directives. If sales people fail, then their management have failed first.

A harsh aspect of this is that the manager who cannot come to grips with this truth is possibly out of place in a management role. The role of the sales manager is not about filling potholes on the sales force organisational chart, it's about building great sales forces, no matter what the environment or product. It's about the ability to attract and identify sound candidates, recruit them and bring about results for the company.

Recruiting is as much about your success as it is about the future employee's. To bring in a successful candidate, you need to be a successful manage

CHAPTER 20:

Induction of Sales Personnel

A professional induction is about creating a positive and motivated sales person who is confident and has the right attitude towards the company and their new role

Many sales managers see the induction process as detracting from their usual work and, therefore, as something of a nuisance. They have their priorities wrong. They dismiss it as being relatively unimportant and delegate the task as often as they can to someone else. In many cases, the new salesperson is not really inducted, but thrown into the deep end and left to fend for themselves. The attitude tends to be that if they're at all capable, they will manage for themselves without a lot of assistance from the company. This shows a lack of understanding of their obligations on the part of the manager. Furthermore, it is a missed opportunity to get the new sales person on track for the company.

Why bother with induction?
Companies with high turnovers or large sales teams are often challenged by induction. In these situations, many people consider the process a waste of time because the continual turnover of personnel means an endless stream of inductions, eating into what they see as valuable 'productive' time. However, this is not the problem; the actual problem stems back to the structure of the position and the recruitment process.

If you remember, in earlier chapters we stressed that your new recruits are your security for the future. If they are successful, then you will be successful. We also touched on the differences in culture between a small business and a franchise. Remember our admonishment not to pay someone to make the mistakes that you have already made? Most readers will agree that there simply is no logic in this. Remember also that what happens even as early as the interview process sets the scene for the successful candidate's employment with your company, so if you are going to take control, do so at the outset. These two points are your strongest argument in favour of the implementation of an induction process for all new members of your sales team. Develop a good, strong formal induction programme and make it work for you - you'll find it's time well invested.

A documented and thorough induction programme will ensure the consistent preparation of each new employee, making sure you develop a solid minimum standard within your team. This is your opportunity to programme the best sales force for the company and for your own personal success - don't miss this chance!

What about existing employees?

Induction is not just for new employees. Where you take over an existing team, you should re-induct all employees reporting to you to ensure that they are all working toward your goals and to company requirements.

When conducting a revolution, the re-induction of your team is vital. You need to be sure they have a thorough understanding of the revolution, and that they are focusing in the direction you want them to take. Again, the way to start is with re-induction.

The Induction Programme

The induction should be conducted in the same manner as any other formal sales training, as a formal programme. Be sure to provide staff with adequate (and appropriate) written material, presented in a folder. The information should be in the format of a manual which contains specific sections written in a clear, concise style so as to ensure all readers can read and digest it easily.

The more detail you document and provide to your new employees, the more easily they will adjust to their new environment. The clearer you make the boundaries, requirements and sales process of the company, the more likely they will succeed.

Don't rush the induction. Too many companies push their new staff through the process, seeing it as a form of 'downtime' because the new staff member is not actually 'working', and therefore not productive. You must remember that what you put into someone slowly will stay there, and what you put in quickly will not. A timetable should be established outlining each day and what the new recruit will be undertaking and the resources that will be required for each element.

Remember that you are carefully programming your new recruit to be a productive member of the company, one who fully understands their role and how to interrelate with other people within the company. Each day of the programme should consist of different activities and different people to work with, as this will keep them fresh and in learning mode.

CHAPTER 21:

Sales Personnel Business Plans

After your new sales person has been working with you for approximately three months, and has an understanding of what is required of them as an employee, the next important step you must take is to have them prepare a personal business plan tailored to their position.

Your objective in the creation of a personal business plan is two fold:

1. You will gain a very clear understanding of how your sales person thinks and operates, permitting you to see the business from their perspective. This, in turn, allows you to clearly pinpoint what it is you want to amend or amplify, and to discuss it with them.

2. You are asking the sales person to consider what they are doing and to find smarter methods for operating in the market. This helps give the person ownership of the role and accountability for the results.

What do you ask for?
Provide only limited guidelines as to what information you want from the sales person and leave them to struggle a little in its preparation. This is not an idle exercise; this technique will give you a strong sense of the extent of their business planning skills.

If you provide your staff with a form to fill in, they won't have any reason to strive for the results you want to see. They will complete any form handed to them robotically, giving no thought to the process. You want a process wherein your staff give full and serious consideration to what they are actually doing.

When you get the plan
When you receive the personal business plan, review it thoroughly prior to speaking with the sales person. Above all, never ask for a business plan and then do nothing with it.

After reviewing it, arrange a time to meet with the sales person to go over it. At your meeting, work your way through each subject, point by point. The sales person should take notes and then go away and finalise the plan. The plan that comes back to you then will be the formal version.

Be sure you encourage your staff, adopting the role of advisor and teacher. Never ridicule anyone. This task is for the purpose of developing the person and helping create a highly valued member of the team who is well respected in the market place.

Successful managers develop template documents to guide people in the development of their sales plans after the initial preparation attempt by the sales person.

This establishes a minimum performance and benchmark of how the plans will be presented.

Above all, these plans must be reviewed every quarter. They are living documents and the guidelines or roadmap to success

CHAPTER 22:

General Motivations in a Sales Force

Maintaining the ongoing motivation of a sales force is a never-ending quandary for management. Many managers believe that if you offer good commissions, then that is all the motivation a good seller needs. However, as SFI found in its research on sales forces, only a very small percentage of sales people actually respond to money as their primary incentive. The overriding element that emerged as the most important issues for these people, over and over again, is security. They want to know they will have a job not just in the short term, but also in the long term.

Sales people must therefore be convinced that the company they work for is dealing honestly with them and genuinely cares for their well-being. And how do you achieve this sense of confidence in your staff? This can only be achieved through effective communication between the management and the sales staff. And this is achieved through the creation and consistent use of open and clear channels of communication and, above all, a clear understanding of the job the person is being asked to do, on both the part of the employer and the employee.

When these essential elements are in place, then you can consider the introduction of other motivations.

The team and its members
Most companies work on the basis of motivating a team of people. This is not always going to be productive as the team is made up of individuals and every single member is different. You must treat them as individuals while promoting a team environment to embrace the need that most people have for security.

The role of the manager is to understand the key motivation of each and every individual and not to treat the staff simply as a group. This is a difficult task, complicated by having to avoid being seen to favour particular individuals. Remember that the clarity with which your motivation is conveyed is critical.

What motivates you?

Different things motivate each person. For one person, it might be family time; such as seeing a child at a special function during school hours; for another it might be the desire to exceed targets; yet another might have a real need for a professional individual relationship with the manager, consulting daily in order to clear the day's events and to get set for the next day. Some people may wish to be more than just an employee of the company, enjoying strong social ties and friendships with work colleagues and becoming involved in social activities through work. Another common motivator is the opportunity to take home awards in the form of material items, such as vouchers from major stores, that can be shared with family or partners.

You will need to identify and note what motivates each member of your team. Then you should use this knowledge carefully to ensure a positive response is obtained from the person - remembering to be careful not to elicit a negative response from other members of the team. The rewards or motivations must always be based on measurable outcomes and other points of which everyone is aware.

You can lead a horse to water, but....

The key to motivation is to understand one critical point, which is that motivation comes from within each person. In other words, motivation is self motivation.

People cannot be motivated unless they want to be. And whether they want to be or not comes down to the attitude of each person. In sales, the degree of motivation of the person is critical to the success of the role. When a person is calling on twelve to twenty-five customers a week, constantly pushing for time and sales, this can be extremely draining, both mentally and physically. To survive in sales, they must be naturally motivated individuals.

Sales managers must play their part by providing stimulation and rewards to those in the team. These must be a combination of incentives that would provide rewards for all the personalities within the team. These cannot just be financial rewards. You must avoid instituting a process wherein one person can win the majority of awards for being the best seller.

A situation of this nature is the most demotivating that people can put into a business. Everyone must know that their effort, if it is genuine, will always be rewarded. At the end of a cycle (half year or yearly), it is fair to nominate an overall winner, but this should not be a regular occurrence. A simple email to that person, acknowledging that they are the top achiever for the month, is motivating enough for those who are driven by results.

The motivating environment

Sales managers must provide an environment that encourages self-motivation. This consists of a good balance of incentives combined with that most important element, open channels of communication and a clear understanding of their role. The more time and effort you put in with each person, the more likely they are to be motivated. Each member of your team will make decisions that will define their level of motivation. Given the appropriate environment, those levels should be high.

When you start building such an environment, each new incentive being offered will generate in your sales staff a series of decisions determining whether they will be motivated or not, and how motivated they will be.

They will ask themselves a series of questions, and where the answers are 'yes', they will motivate. Where the answers are 'no', don't be surprised if not only do you fail to inspire motivation, but in some cases, the level of motivation drops.

What do the staff ask themselves?

Typically, these are the questions they will ask themselves:

- Does more effort ensure a different outcome will be achieved?
- Does more effort require longer working hours?
- Does more effort require additional resources in the company to achieve the desired outcomes?
- Do I have access to those additional resources?
- Is the request for effort realistic with regard to the marketplace?
- Is the request for effort going to provide me with some personal reward?

The answers to those questions will determine whether or not the staff decide to make any degree of effort.

Career stages of sales people

Sales people work through various stages in their careers. This can have an impact on both your recruitment decisions as well as how they function within the company and the team environment. The mix of people you have must be oriented toward your customer base and not toward what you find easy to manage.

The exploration stage

People in this stage are very achievement oriented and require a high level of management and guidance.

Establishment stage

People who are in this phase have decided that sales is the career that they want. They are committed to the job, and to success, and are striving to move into management roles.

Maintenance stage

People in this stage are good to have if you want stability in your team. They are predictable and in most cases, you can rely on the results they will bring in. They have a pattern of behaviour that will not really change, and as long as that pattern meets your requirements, they are good employees.

Disengagement stage

These people are mentally prepared for retirement and have lost all desire to sell. They are usually quite negative in attitude and will often fall back on conversations that harp on 'the old days'.

All teams must consist of a blend of people. It is important for members to understand that just as you deal with a broad group of clients of varying ages and backgrounds, your sales team must be in a position to meet those needs. Cloned sales teams are not recommended!

Another situation you often face as a sales manager is the plateauing in sales people.

Plateauing is stagnation

How do you recognise when one of your staff has reached a professional plateau? The most obvious signs are when a person has lost the desire to continue improving and developing themselves. Traditionally seen in people in the 40 - 50 years age range, in some cases you will see this in younger people.

The cause of plateauing can be a lack of upward mobility, limited opportunities or seeing one's career as being at a standstill. Other reasons can be boredom, a perception that they have been unfairly treated, burnout or satisfaction with their current income levels. Plateauing can also be experienced when a person is promoted beyond their ability and they are unable to make effective decisions or operate effectively. This is often seen to be stagnation.

Some of the symptoms in sales people are:

- Slowing down their prospecting activities
- Working fewer hours
- Lacking energy, time, enthusiasm, creativity, and most of all,
- A sense of humour.

These people delight in the past and resist changes

It is worth remembering that you should regularly and carefully review the incentives and rewards your company provides. However, never forget that the cheapest reward is often the most overlooked -'thankyou'.

CHAPTER 23:

Sales Training

Sales training is something that can be debated by anyone involved in sales. One thing that is common is that people do not realise the full value of training and certainly in Australia and New Zealand sales people have become, without a doubt, some of the most under trained personnel in an organisation over the past few years. Those companies that do excel and achieve strong growth are those that are investing in their people and rate training a high importance.

Unfortunately they would be one in every two or three hundred which is a poor reflection on the career of sales. The companies that struggle in the market, in many cases unnecessarily, rate sales training as a much lower requirement and place more emphasis on product knowledge and long term customer relationships. They do not see any real value in training and work on the premise 'we tried it but it did not work'.

There is a sense amongst managers of whether the investment is really worth it. Some management taking the tack of letting the sales people prove themselves first and foremost, whilst others seeing greater value in training from the outset. Certainly those establishing a training regime from the time a person commences in the role are those that are seeing shorter ramp up times and achieving a much higher return on their investment in shorter time frames.

Which selling style is right
Selling styles have evolved over the years from the traditional heavy closing seller to a more sophisticated and professional consultative or solution seller. Many of the sellers in the market have failed to adapt to those changes necessary over the years and certainly there are different experiences for each customer based on the years of experience of the seller.

Many sales training programmes on offer have also failed to make that transition to meet current market place requirements

The one selling style that has become redundant in the market is that of one referred to as 'relationship selling'. Relationship selling is about focusing on the personal relationship and friendliness of the association and this is a style that is really only suitable for a marketplace that is buoyant and with a much lower level of competitiveness. It provides a shelter for the sales people who are under performing and remove accountability from their role and focus on the softer side of the association with the customer, rather than the over-riding elements of profitability and sales revenue.

What is your selling culture?

All companies have their own preferred selling style, which is usually determined by the current sales manager. Whether that style is a combination of styles that has organically grown within the organisation that has no professional training in place. Or a training system is used to create the culture of the team and the team is seen as a brand in the market. The brand demonstrating the methods and processes they use to be uniform in all personnel.

> *Companies must identify that the most important behaviour that attributes to the success of a sales person is their attitude. The second most important being their selling skills.*

The less training they are provided as a team or as individuals, the less likely they are going to succeed in their role. It impacts on their professionalism, degree of frustration, motivation and their overall likelihood of identifying opportunities. The lack of training will account for many missed opportunities and certainly it cultivates individuals that are focused on the retention of existing business rather than the securing of new business as it's a softer environment to sell in and reduces their frustration and pressure to perform.

With the changes in the economies and the shortage of good sellers and quality personnel to recruit in the market, the need for training is going to be even more amplified over the coming years. Those companies that excel will be those that have invested heavily in their personnel. This will also become a key factor in attracting and retaining good people within your organisation as the employee becomes the one selecting where they will work, rather than the employer having the final selection. The more skill shortage that occurs the more control the sellers will have over their employment selection and criteria for an organisation to meet.

So what training do you embark on?

Certainly sales training has evolved considerably from its humble days of classroom lectures over a number of days. People have learnt, and maybe this is the catalyst to the lack of desire to engage in training, that traditional classroom training over a few days is typically ineffective. People come away with one or two good ideas but certainly not enough information that will support their development and provide the foundations of a professional seller to represent you in the market.

In today's market the training is more sophisticated and online training is becoming the most preferred method of training where individual coaching is part of the online process. As like with all styles of training, online has evolved from simply reading a screen, through to multiple choice questions to a level now where it is about individual coaching of the person by the trainer in the online medium.

The key to success with training is that it must be on-going forming a culture in the business and the basis of how the company communicates both internally and externally.

A contributing factor for the success of any training will come directly from the manager. The degree of follow through and emphasis that is placed on the training information to ensure it is carried through into the customer's environment and experience.

Sales managers must take an approach to training that is going to bring about career development for individuals. A series of programmes, subjects and knowledge references that are going develop the individual over a period of time and establish a benchmark of performance within the team.

The training would be directly linked to the job description to ensure that each person is skilled to perform the task required, and constantly coached to retain that skill level in the market place.

The skill development will not be limited to just sales training. It will be all encompassing including time management, customer service, negotiation skills, tiered selling skills training (referring to inside sales, field sales, major account management) and above all, fundamental business acumen to keep them focused on revenue rather than just relationships. The training should be continual with a minimum of fifteen days formal training per annum and weekly reinforcement to ensure it becomes the culture within the company and establishes the brand and quality of the individual representing the organisation in the market.

Creating a selling culture through training in your organisation will have a positive impact on your financial returns achieved.

When looking to engage in training there are few simple areas that you must review carefully if you are to gain results from your investment.

Does the individual have the right attitude toward training and will they be open minded to learning? If they are not then you should also consider their long term contribution to them being a member of your team.

Is the training addressing behavioural changes through formal competency testing, education and review of training to identify areas of improvement? Certainly behavioural changes cannot be achieved in a few days and it is necessary for the training to be held over several weeks to achieve a degree of success.

Is the training being led by an outstanding person in the field of selling that is going to raise the benchmarks within the team or are you hiring 'like for like'? Are they a person that is going to gain respect and contribute to skill learning or a person that will be disregarded by the participants?

Can you afford to have personnel off the road or are you better placed to take advantage of online training where accessibility is more flexible?

Can you afford to bring the team together for training and meet behavioural changes requirements? Traditionally people have brought teams together for training and team development. They are in fact two different requirements and should not be combined to one as you dilute the effect of the training. Team development is one stand alone requirement, selling skills and related core skills are another requirement.

Is the training going to be individually focused with self paced learning and coaching, or is it group training where individuals are left in a quandary on the elements they have missed. Interestingly, through our own experiences in online training, participants will take up to one third additional time than the actual module time as they replay elements and focus on points that they personally gain value from. They report in a classroom those points would have been lost as the training progresses on to meet the group needs not their individual needs.

The investment in training can be enormous where it is not invested wisely. When invested wisely you can reap enormous benefit both in the individual and the results they achieve.

Buyer beware!

An emerging trend amongst those sales trainers that are struggling to meet the requirements of training in today's market have taken the step of working in the field with the individuals as a method of coaching.

This style of training is fraught with problems as it can have negative impact on the individual and the customer they are calling on if not handled correctly. Rarely have we heard of positive results from a customer's perspective and it arouses suspicion in many situations regarding the sales person's performance.

From a training perspective it is the finishing tool that must be completed by the manager, and not a task that can be delegated. External trainers provide a foundation and method and managers provide the finishing tools of ensuring it is taken to the customer interface.

An interesting point is to remember that during a revolution, the time spent in the field with individuals that are not performing well has been a major tool in removing them from the organisation without issue.

For the manager

As a manager, training has a significant impact on how the team reporting to you performs. It can be the case of a dollar saved today is going to lose you one hundred dollars a day in opportunity being missed.

Companies that do not provide training are hurting themselves financially, as they are not improving and investing in their greatest asset - the sales person, the provider of revenue.

CHAPTER 24:

Field Management

Field management is an area that many managers avoid. Why is this? It could be that field management is extremely time-consuming, and tends to be very intense as you are working one on one with a sales person. Yet this is a management practice that should be viewed as an essential part of your coaching format. In fact, it should be a fundamental element of any work you plan to do with your staff. Handled correctly, it can be the most valuable time you spend in training. It is not a task you can delegate or have an external contractor do for you.

What you see in the field can never be replicated in a formal training situation as it's live, it's real and it consists of a series of different, real-life experiences. Formal training provides structure, process and skill application. Field work is the final and ongoing refinement required.

What does the manager actually do out in the field?
Always remember that the conduct of the manager on these appointments is as critical as the conduct of the sales person. This is an exercise for the sales person, and not an opportunity for the manager to grandstand. This happens more often than people imagine, and completely negates any value in the exercise. Don't make the experience a negative one for your staff; ensure they benefit from it and don't consider these outings with you as an experience to be borne with clenched teeth.

There are few sound rules that go with field management:

1. Do not discredit your sales person in front of the customer by doing all the talking or correcting their errors in the middle of the appointment.
2. Note your observations and work over any issues arising from fieldwork with the person post-appointment. The hardest part of attending appointments as an observer is to listen to errors and not be tempted to resolve them on the spot.

3. Do not let the customer form an association with you. You are the observer and you are there to watch the sales person interact with clients. If you intervene, the sales person will not be able to hold their own with their clients on later visits. Be aware that the customer will always seek to deal with the manager as they are perceived as having the authority to change sales, give discounts etc. Do not succumb to the temptation to participate!

4. If the customer keeps turning to the sales manager for answers ensure you loop the sale back to the sales person during the appointment and close off. Make sure the customer knows whom their contact is. If the customer persists, then perhaps you have spoken too much and have made it difficult for your sales person to take control of the meeting.

Warning

If you don't have good selling skills yourself, then this is not an activity to take on. You'll find yourself in the hot seat and will be expected to have answers to any and all questions. What you teach out in the field will be used, and you have to know it will work.

Why go out on in the field?

The purpose for your trip out into the field with your staff is to observe their conduct and selling techniques and to subsequently critique and train the person. If necessary, you will be trying to change the way they communicate with their clients to help them achieve results for the business. This is a firsthand opportunity to get to the heart of what, if anything, is going wrong, and to help your very successful staff do even better. You may even learn something yourself!

It's in the details...

This style of training is about getting into the micro issues. Communication does not just consist of the sales person's face-to-face encounter with their contacts at their clients' businesses. Communication is in body language, appearance, and comportment. No aspect of their conduct is too trivial for you to consider.

Listen to their sentence structure when they speak, consider the wording they use, and the emphasis they place on specific topics. Observe the methods they use at the sales appointment. Watch closely every aspect of their behaviour, including how they behave in reception, how they conduct themselves walking into offices and into boardrooms. Watch how they initiate conversations with their clients. Every small detail is part of the information that helps you determine whether or not you have a high quality seller representing you in the market place.

Always remember the purpose of this exercise, which is about fine tuning the physical detail. Your staff need to be trained in the details at this point. This exercise is definitely not about the conceptual aspects of selling.

Why aren't the sales converting?

A common (and sometimes harrowing) experience of being a sales manager is the first appointment in field management.

One that stands out in our memory is a trip with a sales person to see a customer located in the suburbs of a major city. The customer was a large organisation with offices in several countries and had been well established for many years. It was a very successful business, with some five hundred employees in the head office alone.

We entered the offices and Tom, our sales person, spoke briefly with the receptionist. He then immediately went over to the reception area couch and flopped down as if he were settling in to watch Sunday afternoon sports at home. In spite of correcting that moment, the walk to the boardroom with the client was a nightmare as Tom started to chat, making obvious and clichéd comments about the offices. On entering the boardroom he immediately sat down, not even thinking of waiting until anyone else was in the room, much less seated. Again, he sprawled, leaning across the boardroom table and pulling out a disreputable-looking old note pad covered with scratchy, meandering notes. This, apparently, was the sum total of what he felt he needed to know from the client. Tom took further notes with an old pen that was obviously a promotional pen from some past event.

The conversation started with him talking about a discussion they had had by telephone. This was followed by a great outburst of what Tom wanted from the company in terms of information and assistance. The customer sat there, obviously wondering why he ever agreed to an appointment with this man, trying to stay focused. As Tom became more excited and voluble, he sprawled further over the boardroom table, pushing his notepad to one side and stretching across toward the customer while making his points. He repeatedly asked the same questions and kept going back to subjects in which the client had clearly exhibited a complete lack of interest.

The closing was a monumental example of everything you shouldn't do in selling. Tom told the client he would get a proposal to him and set a time that was suitable to himself, rather than asking the client if he wanted to know anything further.

The entire appointment consisted of statements and challenges from the sales person. There was simply no give and take, and the talking ratio was ninety percent Tom and ten percent the customer.

On leaving the appointment and being asked how he thought it had gone, Tom said it went well. He was quite excited. Guess who got sold? Tom sold himself, and the poor customer is still sitting there, baffled, wondering what on earth - if anything - happened. We had a lot to talk about in the car.

The interesting point here is that, to varying degrees and in a variety of styles, we have seen this kind of behaviour many times over.

As a manager taking over a new team you have to wonder:

1. How was Tom ever recruited?

2. Why would you pay him so much to be set loose in the market?

3. What quantities of business had he lost due to this unbelievable selling style?

The thought of having one or more staff like this would be overwhelming - imagine the workload ahead of you in order to fix the problems these people create! We often wonder why managers haven't picked up on this appalling behaviour earlier. Surely they have been on appointments with these people to witness this first hand? If not, then they are certainly reducing their chances of success if this is the kind of person they are relying on for sales.

CHAPTER 25:

Performance Reviews

The purpose of a Performance Review is precisely that – to review performance

Performance reviews are something that all managers and personnel prefer to avoid. An exercise in which the performance of staff is reviewed against the expectations of the position, the performance review is usually a two-way process. Employees are asked to assess their own performance and the management provides their assessment of that same performance.

Since the timing of the performance review is usually tied to the salary review cycle, it is not surprising that it is seen as an opportunity for the employee to sell their skills (and the income they generate) to the employer once again, and for the employer to make the person struggle the quest for an incremental pay rise. Given this fairly common perception of the process, it is no wonder that most people see it as having little real value. Most people simply believe that no one benefits from a performance review - neither the company nor the staff member.

Over the years, SFI has seen performance reviews conducted in a wide range of companies, using a variety of methods. The mistake that stands out as most commonly made by many people is that most of these reviews are conducted 'in the grey.' That is, these reviews are conducted with very little structure and not against measurable tasks or duties. This happens when no measurable elements of the person's role are used to define their performance, resulting in a process that is at best subjective because it is basically the sales person's perception pitted against the manager's.

Tighten up those job descriptions
We found that this lack of measurable indicators was linked back to a grey job description (or, in some cases, no job description at all), into which little thought had been put with the result that the duties listed were ambiguous and hard to assess or measure.

For example, 'building customer relationships' is a favourite duty on a position description. This is a perfectly understandable aim for a sales person, but just how do you go about measuring your sales person's success in this area? This is not an easily measured task and, although often phrased in a very authoritative manner, in essence it has very little real meaning.

Opinions regarding the amount of effort that has been put into the customer relationship, or the value of the relationship (particularly when it comes to new business), or the outcome of the relationship building will always differ. All these points are ambiguous and create the potential for arguments or disputes. Obviously the sales person is going to report an enormous workload and, unless the sales report is full of great results, the employer will in turn question and reject many of the statements made by the seller.

We could write volumes on the number of duties in the job descriptions that we have seen that open the door to these very woolly, difficult-to-measure issues. Without specific and quantifiable tasks in the job description, the performance review becomes useless and unfeasible.

Another situation we encountered is that in which key performance indicators are changed throughout the year when new methods of generating figures are adopted. This sort of change frequently causes resentment in employees as, from their perspective, the company usually ends up in a better position than they do. These changes can range from a change in reporting, in accounting or even a territory change. With few exceptions, sales people will take a negative view of the situation.

Who conducts the performance review?
A key to how the performance review will be perceived in your company is the person who conducts them. There are various schools of thought on this issue. One popular theory is that the person who conducts the review should not be directly involved in managing the staff member being reviewed. The reasoning behind this is that this ensures the process can be objective and the 'outsider' brings a fresh perspective to the process.

We have seen some interesting pairings as a result of this theory - accountants conducting reviews of sales people, sales managers conducting reviews of production personnel. Our observation is that, more often that not, this creates a negative situation in which the employee may actually take the opportunity to complain about their own management rather than bringing something constructive to the process.

Best results are achieved if the person's direct manager conducts the performance review. The quality of the job description and the key performance indicators will define the quality of the performance review.

How often should we review performance?

Many companies have in place an annual cycle for performance reviews. In our experience, this is not an effective system. If you look at the performance review process as one that is flexible and adaptable, then you will see how easily it can be used in different forms and at different levels.

To manage a successful sales team the performance review process should be used in various forms throughout the year. The most successful sales teams adopt this system; the outcomes bear witness to its sense. You will find that the once-a-year process is used by average or non-performers.

Staging of Performance Reviews

Stage One - weekly sessions

Each week you should conduct a one-on-one performance review with each member of your team. This is a brief and informal process, and you should take notes as needed for action points or follow-up.

What you are asking your sales people to do is to provide you with a weekly report of their achievements and what they have planned for the coming week. This means you are keeping close to their individual performance and have a hands-on understanding of the issues they are dealing with throughout each week.

This level of personal attention builds great respect between sales people and their managers. A common reaction to this method is that it takes too much time or its micro-management. Without the sales plan in place it could be perceived as micro-management, however in the early stages of their employment the more attention provided the more success both the employee and the company will enjoy. The returns are so great that no manager can afford not to do it.

Stage Two - the quarterly review
Each quarter, conduct a formal performance review.

The most professional reviews are conducted in accordance with each of the specific requirements of the job description and key performance indicators. Where the sales person has an individual sales plan, the review will have even more value and purpose.

Stage Three - the annual review
The annual performance review is linked to the salary review. Inevitably, if the company follows the three-stage review process, then this annual review will be less daunting for both the sales person and the manager. By the time the annual review rolls around, the manager will have conducted weekly and quarterly reviews of staff performance and all staff should have a company sense of where they stand and what is required of them.

What are the benefits of the review?
When used as an ongoing tool, the Performance Review will benefit the company and its staff by:

- providing an analysis of business plans to performances
- developing strategies for improvement
- airing and settling company-related problems
- airing and settling personnel-related problems
- resolving conflicts

Certainly in organisations where we have implemented or the management of implemented this regime of reviews, there has been a significant increase in not only the sales results being achieved, but moreover in the employee satisfaction with their role. They have clarity over what is required and are clear on the areas of their performance they are excelling and also area where they need to attribute more attention. The communication and respect between employer/employee or manager/employee is greatly enhanced and there is a greater sense of team in the organisation.

Over a twelve month period of time the business will evolve its skill level establishing a higher benchmark of minimum performance which further contributes to sales growth.

CHAPTER 26:

Sales Meetings

Same old, same old

Sales meetings are, without doubt, one of the most painful experiences a sales person will ever sit through. And all sales managers have sales meetings; it is well-known of the industry. Why, then, do we continue to tolerate these boring and dreary events, most of which accomplish little and simply drift from one week to the next?

Let's consider a typical sales meeting scenario: the manager reviews the team's performance and either belts them around or over-praises what is, essentially, an average job done. The manager might then talk about some new product, perhaps raise certain problems and offer solutions for other areas in the business. This may have some productive aspects to it, but on the whole, sales meetings are boring and a waste of time.

And how long do these ordeals generally run? Meetings can take from one to three hours, depending on how much the manager wants to drive home a point and how much of a working-over the team is going to get.

So why have a sales meeting at all?

What is the purpose of a sales meeting, then? Sales meetings are actually training and development forums and should not just be the standard (read dreary) meeting that you run each week or month. They should have a format threaded through them over the course of the year, ensuring that all team members are being developed and that their focus is on the objectives of the company.

And to be effective, sales meetings should be conducted weekly. If you run a decentralised team, conference calls work very well.

Remember that the sales meeting is a forum, and an opportunity for give and take in terms of information and feedback. All members of the team should benefit and all should be able to participate freely.

Each manager should develop their sales meeting planner for up to twelve months in advance and establish the dates up to three months in advance. Ensure the sales planner includes how you are going to develop the team and what value the participants are going to get out of attending the meeting.

CHAPTER 27:

Counselling Staff

Why counsel?
Sometimes a staff member's service performance or attitude is substandard. In order to bring about improvement, the manager needs to discuss the problem with the staff member. Unfortunately, not all managers find this easy for a variety of reasons.

Lack of assertion skills
Culturally, we are discouraged from asserting ourselves. For individuals not accustomed to doing so, confronting a situation of this nature is very difficult.

Dislike of confrontation
In this sort of situation, most people will hope that the problem will simply go away as almost no one likes confrontation. But ignoring the problem will only make it get bigger, and more severe.

Don't want to be 'the heavy'
Again, it's easier to be everyone's friend. Discussing poor performance or an attitude problem is not likely to endear you to anyone. But it needs to be done.

Fear of damaging friendships with staff and an uncomfortable atmosphere
This is related to the reluctance to play the 'heavy'. No one likes to be the bearer of bad tidings. But the situation only worsens if it is left to fester, so it is best to do something as quickly as possible. As for creating an uncomfortable atmosphere, that is far more likely to be the result of an unresolved problem, affecting not only your relations with the person in question, but other members of the team as well, if not the entire team.

Reluctance to come to grips with problems which may be embarrassing to either/both parties

People will do a lot to avoid a potentially embarrassing situation. This is where your interpersonal skills come to the fore. You must be able and willing to handle any staff situation. If you foresee embarrassment, consider strategies to minimise that aspect of the session.

Remember, any behaviour you accept, you automatically condone

Always take action because, if you say nothing, you actually reinforce the unacceptable behaviour, which then infects other personnel.

CHAPTER 28:

Coaching

Although management styles have come a long way in the last two decades, the command and control style of management behavior remains common practice in many sales units. It can be directly seen as command style or be camouflaged behind the autonomous mantra where people are just expected to their job with little input from management. In controlling management styles, the manager is in charge, has all the answers, and fixes all the problems.

In the first style, the control aspect is vocal, and they will demonstrate this style through either commanding every move of the people (a little military style) or alternatively by letting the salespeople run free and waiting for mistakes where they can take the hero status of fixing them. They are the people with all the answers that fix all the problems. You will also see a reflection of this in how they deal with customers, as they seek to be the firefighter-problem solver for customers, too.

It's no surprise that plenty of people find this approach demotivating, and that workplaces with a command-control style are rated as unsatisfying. When people feel as though they have no say and are given no opportunity to contribute, then they switch off and become "disengaged."

The manager now must take a coaching approach or be a manager-coach.

The sales manager's ability to coach his or her team is one of the most important aspects of the position. As sales manager, you need to be able to work with your team in order to continually build their results and performance. Make coaching an integral part of your management style.

Why do people defer coaching?

Even though the benefits of coaching have been very clearly demonstrated again and again over the years, people in positions of authority still tend to put off these sessions. With everything else the busy sales manager has to do in a week, it is easy to feel they don't have the time for these 'frills'. But it is important to understand that coaching, like counselling, is not an 'extra'; it is an essential part of the well-managed sales team.

A common problem is that many sales managers simply don't have coaching skills - no one has ever actually taught them. They fob off the activity by saying that the company's standards are obvious, and staff should know what to do without needing even more of the manager's time giving them pep talks. But coaching is essential - it is a way to address a situation before letting it get out of hand.

When is coaching useful?

Coaching is a technique that is used when inducting a new employee. Most people coach, whether they know it or not, in this situation. It is also a very good tool when you are teaching a new on-the-job skill to existing personnel. And it is a very efficient way to make simple corrections to performance.

Another valuable use of coaching is as follow up to a formal training session. It is not enough to send staff to training, or to run training sessions, and then just let them get on with it - you must reinforce the principles and skills taught at training in an ongoing manner, and coaching is the perfect means for doing this.

CHAPTER 29:

Exit Interviews

A great deal can be learned from staff as they are exiting employment with your company. The compulsory conducting of exit interviews can be a great source of information for the continuous improvement of the company.

What can be gained from the exit interview?
An exit interview is a time when the employee who is leaving the company is guided through a series of questions, with the intention of eliciting certain information from that person. The aim of the exercise is to tap into their view of the business, regardless of whether the person has resigned voluntarily or been dismissed. This is beside the point; both parties can gain much by the exit interview and it should be held.

Why so many people don't hold exit interviews
Let's face it, nine times out of ten, a person who is leaving is disgruntled, at the very least, or he/she would not be leaving the company, right? And if you give that person a formal opportunity to explain why he/she is leaving, you're basically just opening the door to a stream of complaints or abuse. Right?

Wrong.

This is certainly not the experience of SFI with exit interviews, or at least not with most. Unfortunately, most people are afraid to test this statement. They believe people will exploit the situation and make things very difficult at worst, and at best, say nothing useful. Don't sit still for this; design an exit interview process that gets you every last possible grain of information that you can use to improve your company.

A lot of information can be gleaned from these interviews and they are well worth holding. The way to minimise the potential for a negative experience is to structure the exercise appropriately for maximum gain and minimum pain. Even with an axe to grind, most people respond well to being treated well, and if you show the person being interviewed that you respect his/her opinion, in most cases that person will reward you by serious consideration of your questions and a well thought-out response.

The interviewer

Just as the performance review should not be conducted by anyone other than a person's direct supervisor, someone other than the person's direct supervisor should conduct the exit interview. This is because you are trying to get real information, based on fact, and an exit interview with a person who does not directly supervise the person is likely to be less emotional and more factual. However, bear in mind that emotions may enter into the situation even so, and it is important to ensure the person (with some guidance to keep the interview on track) has their say, so don't limit the length of the interview. The interview should allow the employee to state fully what is on their mind.

What should be asked in an exit interview?

It is useful to have a proper format for the interview. This means that the interviewer has a structure to follow and can easily convey to the interviewee that it is a formal process, not a free-for-all. This makes it easier to steer the interview along a predetermined course and gently nudge the departing employee, should emotions threaten to hijack the process, back on course.

Take notes as the comments you elicit can be very useful, but do stress to the interviewee that you are only recording these to help you remember the comments.

In cases where animosity has developed during the period of employment and was not resolved satisfactorily, strive to conclude the exit interview on as positive a note as possible.

What then?

Now the interview is over, the person has left ... what remains to be done? Well, you've received some very interesting information. Use it positively. Analyse it, get a sense of the validity of the opinions expressed. If some suggestions have been offered about the induction process, go back and see if that process can be improved. Never walk away from the exit interview without giving serious consideration to what you have learned. The key here, as ever, is to follow up.

EPILOGUE

As you reach near the end of this book, you will have gained a greater insight into what is required to achieve significant increases in sales and combat the changing markets that we work in from year to year. You will be able to map a direction of what you need to have in place, what is the best route for your business and who are the vehicles to use to ensure results at the end of the day.

You will have been able to analyse your business and management against those of other companies. You may have even related to some of the stories contained throughout the book. These stories are unfortunately not abnormal and the experience many companies (both directors and employees) endure. The case studies following will also assist you in understanding some of the road ahead for you.

Throughout this book there has been continual evidence of the need for companies to rethink and revolutionise their sales forces and sales results. The expectations of the past are changing as the level of accountability and performance standards within the selling function is increasing.

If we continue to adopt those practices from the past or make only minor changes from those practices, your company or employment is operating at threat. At best, consider if you are doing the same thing in twelve months' time from reading this book, you have ultimately missed the opportunity and are now flagging well behind your competitors.

The sales aspect of a business is being rationalised. Not through cost cutting but through a management style that looks at the systems, the detail and the micro issues of producing results. This is a new era in management that will certainly see a sorting of both companies and their management as they are faced with the challenge of producing results in shorter time frames.

There are new skill bases to be learnt, new mind sets of priorities and what is acceptable.

To go down the journey of a revolution is both exciting and profitable to the companies, as long as they can endure the pain and condense it into short and specific time frames. It is not a course of action you practice on. It is not a course of action you just stop midway. It is about dedication to the end result through persistency and consistency.

The ability to step outside the business and work the changes from the outside is critical, to ensure commercial approaches and not emotive, and to clearly negate the past practices that are capping the earnings of the business.

We hope the information within this book has the positive impact on your bottom line that it has had on many organisations that have already taken that bold step and increased their business results significantly.

If you would like the full complete information on sales force management we recommend you complete the Mastering Sales™ Team Management Programme.

If you are interested in sales force development please contact Adele Crane at Sales Focus International.

Contact details are at the back of this book.

CASE STUDIES

Each of the case studies here has been put together to provide readers with an insight into the experiences of other companies. We have selected a group of five studies that most closely describe situations commonly experienced by many organisations. We have not focused on the successful, but rather, on the unsuccessful, which examples provide a very strong learning process for readers of this book. We have provided one excellent success story, which we feel gives a good example of what it takes to achieve a successful revolution.

From this cross section you will be able to gain invaluable insight into what is and what is not required if you are going to develop your company successfully.

For those people looking to transform a business in the capacity by way of a Revolution, please take particular note of how you can overcome some of the barriers that you will experience.

All the companies in these case studies identified the need to change. All gave consideration to the need for change based on their background experience and trading.

On reading these studies you will be amazed at how logic flies out the window in the face of adversity, and how some businesses literally trade into failure because of their inability - and unwillingness, to follow a logical, well thought out process.

CASE STUDY

The Disappearing Managing Director

Company	Name withheld
Industry	Information technology
Structure	National company, division of a multi-national organisation
Number of Managers	Sixteen in total including managing director, general manager and line managers for each business unit/state
Managing Director	Background of strategic and accounting
Number of Staff	approximately 150
Turnover	$24,000,000 pa (pre-tax profit year $500,000)

Profile

The company was a well-known corporation with a good reputation for delivery of services offered. It had been in the Australian marketplace for a number of years and was part of a number of mergers and acquisitions during its growth periods. It had begun to experience problems due to stagnating revenue and increasing overheads. Heavily driven by direct marketing, there was little outbound selling through either call centre or account manager activities. The management wanted the company to reduce its direct marketing activity and evolve to a more sales activity based company.

Company Culture

As a result of a series of acquisitions and mergers, the company was quite diverse in culture, with pockets of the various old companies that had been merged. There was evidence of only a little work done on merging cultures. There was a lack of system and process and what they did have, related to the adaptations of each merger.

The company operated on low accountability within its business units and no action was taken over instances of non-performance. The relationships between employees took a higher priority than sales within the team and the company. The decision making process was slow and many decisions were delayed for long periods of time. Each business unit manager supported the non-performance of other managers.

Due to a high turnover in staff, which is common in merger environments, the company placed a strong emphasis on human resource-related issues rather than on sales focused issues. Following a board meeting, it was announced at senior management level only that due to company's financial position they had under six months to produce the necessary results to their board. The sales division would be closed if improved sales figures were not produced by the time of the mid-year report.

Objective

The company decided to become sales focused, recognising the need to offset the downward trend they were experiencing. A new approach that would reprioritise people's thoughts and behaviour was required, meaning undergoing significant change. This would occur from re-education of the management team, implementation of systems and methods to provide structure to guide the internal and external sales force. The sales force would be trained and developed as an on-flow of the other changes. Direct marketing was to be reduced and all activity within the company was to support a new sales-based culture.

Operating Issues

During the development of the business unit managers, one of the most astonishing facts that came to light was that they had no idea whatever of their daily, weekly takings. They had not even considered having such information reported to them. Their normal course had been to respond to reports provided to them, rather than sourcing the information themselves.

The business unit managers made no conscious effort during their time with the company to review the revenue returns from each person contributing to the team. They based all sales figures on monthly team contributions. There was a high degree of 'lay blame and justify' whenever questions that required an answer about their performance standards or contributions were asked.

The company was excessively focused on cost centres and profitability, although there was no process or method in place to increase the revenue of the business. Nor were there any real measurement formats in place to understand return on investment of marketing dollars spent. The sales people were not accountable for sales results and no action was taken for under performance. No sales people in the state teams were achieving budgets, and all results were measured as team contributions. The team as a whole was some 30% under budget.

The customer listing reflected that 95% of accounts (some 2500 in total) failed to meet the minimum criteria requiring an account manager to call on them. The company was achieving only minimal sales from companies, proving that they were seen as a fall back position for purchasing rather than as a priority supplier.

During the education process, many areas of the business were identified as problem areas. The line managers were challenged senior management, and were required to adopt new practices. Each person was required to adopt certain behaviours within specified time frames to produce results at both an activity and sales results level. The managing director conveyed his desire for this to be followed through and sought commitment from all concerned.

The impact of the change was felt in the state offices within two weeks of the education process with various responses. Some responded with positive results and others sought refuge in human resource-related issues. No counselling was provided to individuals, although this could have provided continual refocusing on the need for a sales-based culture when human resource issues were raised.

The company achieved results in many areas with some business units reporting increases in sales of up to 100% on their previous weeks, and continually growing. An energy developed in the business. Where the focus was selling, the results continued to climb.

However, the managing director was conspicuous for his absence from all senior management discussions in the two months following the initial development. He did not reinforce the change process, and delegated that responsibility to the newly appointed general manager who was promoted from within the business to carry out the changes.

Although he was present during the briefing, education and debriefing processes in which it was highlighted the need to resist altering any of the new systems and methods for a period of six months, the general manager elected to change some of the measurement systems and reinforcement processes.

Furthermore, his appointment was politically loaded, and several senior members of the company had voted a lack of confidence due to his previous poor performance in other businesses. This resulted in several senior management team members departing, including the national sales manager and the national marketing manager.

Several of the newly appointed state business managers were forced out of the business by the general manager because of the disturbance of the existing culture and relationships even while previously non-performing units were exhibiting increased sales figures. The remaining managers were not comfortable with the changed focus of results. The general manager told them that relationships were a major priority in the business.

Identified Problems

- There was a lack of commitment from the managing director and key players. They did not recognise the depth of their problems and what was required to bring the business back to a profitable situation. This resulted in inconsistency in their reinforcement of the procedures and methods, and a reliance on the verbal agreement to change rather than evidential change.
- The general manager lacked experience to manage multiple sites and did not understand the need to retain the consistency and structure put in place at the commencement of the change process.
- The staff contributed to all decisions and changed the measurement systems to reduce their effectiveness and focus on other issues in the business.
- The relationship issues were prioritised over and above the business' fundamental requirements of growth and profitability.
- The business was managed through collaborative decisions rather than leadership.

Outcome

After several months of sales increases in various states, the business failed to perform overall and has been withdrawn under the umbrella of another profitable division of the company, with partnering or outsourcing of many services to reduce cost exposures. The sales problem was never resolved. The managing director resigned before the merger decision was announced.

CASE STUDY

The Business On the Dole (unemployment benefits)

Company	Name withheld
Industry	E-commerce
Ownership	Government organisations and several IT companies
Structure	State based business delivering on a national basis
Number of Managers	CEO & CFO and three business unit managers
Managing Director	Systems analyst
Number Of Staff	20 people
Turnover	$2 million plus government funding to cover losses

Profile

The company was a government-funded initiative that had been operating for a period of five years. They had developed a series of services to the e-commerce environment and over a period of five years had also worked on other projects that had been dropped due to a total lack of viability. The company based its development on a knowledge pool of employees that were ex-university staff and government personnel. They had incurred considerable levels of debt in spite of the funding, and were facing closure due to their inability to meet minimum commercial requirements. The business was in steady decline for a period of nine months even with government funding supporting it.

Company Culture

The company had undergone considerable change in its short life span due to continual shifts in product focus and direction. In the early years, the focus was product development with little emphasis on commercial requirements and in the later years the emphasis changed due to the pending end of government funding under the initial arrangement. The culture of the company was based on exhibiting knowledge, and not the adoption of common commercial practices used in organisations without this kind of funding.

Elements of the final products on offer were viable in the marketplace while others completely lacked commercial delivery. The overheads of the company were extremely high in comparison to commercially-based competitors, even after cost cutting exercises were conducted.

There was an overall lack of accountability in the business and people were focused on their own education, with no emphasis whatever on sales. A general report was circulated stating that they did not consider they needed sales people, as people would come to them for their knowledge and expertise.

There was a high incidence of closed-door conversations on a one-on-one basis and a very poor culture of jostling for other positions within the business. As a company, they did not communicate in a traceable manner, i.e., email, letters etc. within the company. Everything was verbal and usually in one-on-one environments. Open meetings were frowned upon. Only presentations to staff took place in open environments where attempts were made to provide positive feedback; and the staff knew otherwise.

The company was held at ransom by two sales people who had extensive client relationships developed from an 'old boys' network'. They had been with the business since its early days and had not recorded any client contact details, nor developed any databases other than those products sold. Both had degrees in management and marketing.

Decision

The company recognised the need to change their behaviour due to the pressure of time before government funding expired, and the need to achieve sales results. Senior management had to show its board that action had been taken and results were achievable in order to secure a further payment from the government. The company engaged in a sales development forum to improve the overall returns of the business and provide the requirements for funding.

Operating Issues

Two individuals, the CEO and CFO, led the company and reported directly to the board. These two people were opposing personalities who were in conflict over the best course of action for the business. Their conflict resulted in the CEO resigning (or being overthrown).

The product delivery personnel were nominated as specialists in the field. These people were not willing to be questioned on their product delivery or propositions. On receiving direct feedback from potential customers that they had failed to communicate in a way that gave them an understanding of the service on offer, they simply refused to accept the criticism.

The two existing long-term sales people were held up as successful sellers even though they had failed to sell at even break-even levels to the company's cost requirements.

The sales reports included a probability factor of what they considered would come to fruition. This included probability from the commencement of discussions with a customer versus probability on proposals. There was no commercial basis to these reports and each month their unreliability was established with only some 50% of the prediction coming in. The conversion rates varied month to month.

The end of month sales report included 'accruals'.

On being asked to explain what differentiated their product from that of their competitors, the 'experts' were unable to come up with any differences or added value that they could deliver.

There was no database of the contacts that the sales personnel had made and all sales were dependent on the 'old boys' network' rather than fundamental selling processes.

The long-term sales people were advised by the CFO that they were not required to report to the new sales manager. The new sales manager was there for the newer people only.

The company had assigned only fifty accounts for each sales person to focus on. At the time of assignment, each of these accounts was unqualified and based on brand name only.

The competitor analysis failed to actually identify genuine services delivered by competitors and they had no real understanding of their position in the market. Many of the nominated competitors were not actually competing in the same market!

The pricing system used was based on its cheapest competitor (who was a disgruntled ex-employee of the business who had started up a business in competition with them). Beating that particular company became their primary focus. To achieve this, they were selling at 70% under cost of sale. As a company they saw no problem with this.

Delivery people were heavily involved in the sales process, from initial meeting through to final delivery. The writing of all proposals was done by delivery people with very little input by the sellers.

The company was resource hungry and in many cases there would be five people involved in a process that would normally involve only two in a commercial selling situation. When documentation was required for presentation to the potential customer, the process from meeting to presentation would take up to five-six days, with numerous people involved. The sales process usually required several telephone calls and appointments to get the actual proposal-writing phase completed. The average sale was only $5,000.

Identified Problems

- There was a lack of accountability at senior management level and a high degree of maverick behaviour, with each person believing they could do each task with better results.

- The company employees were focused on their own education of themselves and others rather than the commercialisation of the products.

- They sought to retreat by selling to universities and government rather than commercial businesses.

- The CFO had not identified the genuine cost of sale appropriately and all sales were being made at well under cost. This practice was endorsed even when the information was to hand.

- All decisions were agreed to face-to-face and immediate alternative action taken once outside the room. There was no consistency in communication from management, both in day-to-day activities and in overall direction.

- The company sought refuge in the long-term sales people when under pressure, even after identifying that they were a problem and had to be removed.

- The company was unable to adapt to change, even though it was a young business. It sought guidance from those within the company rather than external experts, even though they market this as being a fundamental requirement for success with their own products.

Outcome

The company is being managed through its original processes, even though these traded them into their problems. This includes having selling under cost of sale accepted as good behaviour. They have secured further government funding and guarantee of all debts to be paid by the funding organisations.

They experienced further resignations of front line personnel, leaving their two long-term field sales people to produce results. Other key delivery personnel within the company also resigned.

At the time of writing this book further resignations were received in various areas of the business, the self appointed sales manager (being one of the longer standing sales personnel) sacked his co-worker of similar longevity, the new CEO went on holidays and general unrest remained with the other personnel. There was no evidence of the business having developed the ability to survive without 'being on the dole'.

CASE STUDY

Getting Your Priorities Right

Company	Name withheld
Industry	Financial services
Structure	National company with centralised services and overseas offices
Number of Managers	Managing director, general manager and business unit managers
Managing Director	Chartered accountant
Number Of Staff	Approximately 50
Turnover	Withheld

Profile
The company had been built over a period of twenty years by an entrepreneurial managing director. The business was in a niche industry that provided them with good access to potential sales and they had developed working alliances that delivered a quality product and return on association to the client base. The business was developed on the basis of sharing of wealth with all members of the company and by providing people with the opportunity to grow and expand within the company.

Company Culture
The company culture was based on the principle that good performers would be rewarded and a high degree of autonomy had developed over a number of years. This was particularly evident in each of the international operations. In those areas, the business was built on the personal interpretation of the people employed. The business was measured on financial performance and was always very profitable which gave room for a management practice of this kind.

Decision
The managing director identified the need for a more consistent and streamlined approach to the selling function of the business, particularly in light of the growth and opportunity in the overseas offices.

Operating Issues

The existing sales people were extremely overpaid for their performance and were not measured by any method other than sales results at the end of the month. They had been with the company for many years and were part of its fabric.

The company was involved in a strategic alliance that provided an outstanding supply of leads to sales people. However, because these people were complacent after many years in the business, they had not pursued many of those opportunities. They relied on the people who rang them directly.

The autonomy of the managers had allowed them to develop significantly different business unit conduct, which was reflected in the fluctuating results from the units.

There was considerable reliance on the managers' verbal representation, which led to senior management being misinformed as to the general status of the operations. This occurred primarily in business units that were low performers and that provided small returns to the company. Priority was placed on those units returning the high values.

The managing director commanded a high degree of respect and loyalty from his personnel and was able to communicate the hard issues to his staff.

The business was developed on commercial decision-making processes (not emotive) where they openly acknowledged they were there to make money, but everything was shared with everyone in the business contributing.

The managing director was dedicated to the outcome of the change process and remained focused, even during the thorniest moments, to ensure the outcome was achieved in a reasonable time frame. He never put an individual's woes, however justifiable, over the commercial requirements of the company. He did not let any individual undo the business. He conducted the process with utmost clarity, never permitting this most important process to be mired under gossip and game playing. For example, if anyone complained about anyone else, that complaint was sent directly to the subject of the complaint for the response. There were few political problems in the business and the result was that everyone benefited.

New sales people, better able to embrace the alliance opportunity, were employed. New systems were installed and there was a general overall emphasis on the selling function.

Identified Problems

- There was a sense of complacency in the business due to the longevity of the employees.
- Systems had not been implemented previously because it was a smaller operation and they placed no real emphasis on international sites. They were seen as long shots.
- The business lacked a sales plan for the development of sales.
- There was a lack of consistency in the selling function from site to site due to the autonomy of the management.

Outcome

The company has achieved significant growth in sales and has a common method of management in the selling function. Sales growth was reported to be over 500% for the same period on the previous year.

The business has embraced the changes and the dedication of the managing director & general manager and the commercial focus of the business were the direct contributors to the outcome.

CASE STUDY

When There is Too Much Growth

Company	Name Withheld
Industry	Software
Structure	State Based company delivering nationally & Asia
Number of Managers	Two directors and line managers
Managing Director	Software Developer
Number of Staff	12 people
Turnover	$3,500,000

Profile

The company developed a software product that was marketed to a niche market. They also imported an American product for delivery to the same market which provided a more up to date version of their software. The company was well known in the market place and ranked approximately third or fourth in product quality. They were focused on customer service and the delivery of a quality product. There was a strong focus on product development and they had employed a series of developers to assist in the task. They had secured some overseas contracts in Asia.

Company Culture

The company culture was atypical of a software development company. They were easily sidetracked into the development of new products or upgrades of existing products. The company had undergone considerable downsizing to reduce costs and it retained an equal balance of sales to delivery personnel. The company was sluggish in its approach to the market and the sales people were producing only limited results with limited effort. They expended energy into the Asian market place but were unable to secure sales in a prime interstate territory.

The sales manager had no formal training in sales or management and came from a product based background. The accountants were heavily involved in the management of the financial aspect of the business and had streamlined costs as effectively as possible. There were some cash flow issues due to the background of the business.

Decision

With the need to control expenditure in hand, the decision was made that they needed to focus the existing sales people on more selling and on improving the overall performance of the business. They had identified the sales people required training and guidance. The sales manager also required education in sales management methods.

Operating Issues

The sales people all came from an engineering background with sound technical knowledge. They were able to communicate with the customers, although they did not have an understanding of the sales process.

There were no real reporting systems in place for the sales people and the company relied only on the financial sales report. It was unable to identify what effort was required to make sales.

Reporting systems, including a pipeline, were established, which gave immediate day to day reference of sales and potential sales with accuracy. The probability factors were removed.

The marketing in the business had been done with banner marketing and media releases and very little had been done in direct marketing to the client base. A marketing campaign was conducted with an immediate positive response in sales.

The support hotline was channelled into one person in the business. This was an extremely technical person who extended telephone calls well beyond the callers' requirements. As the person was well liked by callers, this service remained the same and overflow was directed to a new recruit.

A new customer service person was employed for the purpose of servicing and cross selling and this person made strong contributions to product sales and client care levels.

Interstate sales were handled through trips to customers on a frequent basis and building of relationships and contacts within that state. A strong awareness campaign was conducted in that state to underpin the sales people's activities.

All sales related personnel were educated in the sales process and management process.

Identified Problems

- This company was typical of companies developed from a technical product base. The product was sound in its delivery but sales was an unknown area to them.
- The recruitment of the sales manager was carried out without a real awareness of what constitutes a successful sales manager. The appointee was a very nice person - but definitely out of his depth.
- The directors of the business found sales to be a problem area of the business and made no attempt to learn the fundamentals of sales management. They delegated the task completely - and regrettably - to the wrong person.
- Sales people were employed based on their educational background. No recruitment process was in place to test sales skills or the ability to produce revenue for the company.

Outcome

The business achieved strong sales results and increased in accordance with the company's expectations. The company was not prepared for the growth and struggled with delivery of product due to their cash flow issues.

Results were a 400% increase in productivity of sales personnel and 180% increase in sales.

The existing sales manager was unable to sustain the business after a period of four to five months, as he did not have the skill base or experience to adjust to the demands of the market place. He also had no one with whom to discuss issues as the directors were unable to provide feedback on or analysis of sales related situations.

The sales in the business fell after several months but have been sustained at a profitable level to the business. Enormous opportunity was still available to them but they continue to operate at a level that is comfortable for the directors.

The company experienced too much growth, which created other strains on the business, so the directors elected to sustain it at a level that was comfortable all round, even at the cost of extra profit to them.

CASE STUDY

Old Habits Die Hard at the Top

Company	Name withheld
Industry	Hospitality
Structure	One site
Number of Managers	Managing director & general manager
Managing Director	Businessman
Number Of Staff	Approximately 40 including casual staff
Turnover	$1,500,000

Profile

This business was purchased during a downturn in the economy and was seen as a good investment for the future. Considerable upgrading of the facilities was done to turn it into a well-presented property. The business had a uniqueness in the market place, and provided a range of services including catering to conferences and weddings, as well as its restaurant, hotel and sports activities. None of the owners were on site; they visited on Tuesdays only and the rest of the business was conducted through telephone reports and financial returns.

Company Culture

The company operated on a low level of accountability and its systems did not capture the information required for the cross checking of performances. There was a higher than normal degree of theft on the property and people took extreme liberties in this unmanaged environment. The general manager's verbal representations were relied upon even though he exhibited the same behaviour as the personnel. He took many liberties in his role, and his credentials had not been thoroughly checked.

The owners of the business were extremely wealthy business people and resolved problems by throwing money at them. Their attitude was to try to send the problem away rather than deal with its cause.

The managing director did not possess good people skills, even though he had purchased a 'people business'. He opted to operate away from the site and concentrate on his other major business holdings.

The business was not achieving results and although it was busy, its sales were not covering costs.

Decision

The business required new management on a day-to-day basis and the decision was made to approach a corporate business profile rather than another hospitality based person. The only brief provided was to raise the level of sales and profitability.

Operating Issues

The business was sold out twelve months in advance with sales that averaged out to under twenty-five dollars per head including alcohol for all conferences and events. The market price in the region was around sixty dollars per head plus alcohol. Their pricing was below what it cost to deliver, and was the result of too many freebies being handed out.

The staff were observed stealing unashamedly, taking whole sides of meat, vegetables and other food items, cash from the tills, meals, alcohol and even linen from housekeeping.

A number of managers were scattered throughout the business units, all pulling in different directions, with different approaches to the conduct of the business as a whole.

The staff were downsized from over one hundred and ten people, including casuals, to forty people, including casuals. In spite of the huge reduction in staffing levels, services were still delivered.

Under the old regime, a weekly meeting had been conducted with each full time person in the business, giving him or her the opportunity to raise any issues. The managing director had initiated this meeting format so that he could hear what the issues were. He sought collaborative solutions to problems rather than providing leadership. As they were not productive, these meetings were cancelled.

A new forum was established for complaints and issues, and the new general manager conducted the meetings, keeping things focused in the right direction.

Performance measurement systems were put in place throughout the business to ensure all information was captured, identifying problem areas and what action could be taken to rectify them. All systems were cross-referenced for validity.

A professional seller was employed with the charter to renegotiate existing sales to a level of an average of fifty four dollars per head without alcohol, sustain sales at those levels, and to ensure all venues were fully booked.

The returns from the business changed to reflect the increase in pricing and the acceptance level was higher than at the lower rates. There was no actual change in the cost of delivery to the business, it was just how it was packaged and received.

A large direct marketing campaign was undertaken to increase awareness and interest in the property. This saw many major corporations become clients of the business.

Identified Problems

- There was no accountable management on the premises to ensure performance
- The quality of full time personnel was low and the company had no professional recruitment programme
- The lack of thoroughness in the managing director's behaviour was reflected in his personnel
- The managing director was not seen as a leader as he used collaborative decision-making processes - he did not have his staff's respect
- Verbal representations were relied upon too heavily, to the detriment of the business
- No genuine selling effort was made - what effort was made was a default activity of some of the personnel
- The employees were very busy doing basically nothing due to lack of system, procedure and direction

Out*come*

The business was increased 400% in ten months for comparison to the same period in the previous year. The profitability increased dramatically within this growth.

The managing director reinstated the Tuesday meeting concept within two days of SFI relinquishing control of the site. He relied on the verbal representations of the people in the business as he considered he should not have to double-check their performances. He believed that as professionals, this was unnecessary. Unable to break away from old habits, even after acknowledging they were the root of the problem, the company failed rapidly.

The business has now been leased out as the Managing Director was unable to continue to achieve results and it quickly traded back into a loss situation.

REFERENCE MATERIAL OF SURVEY

Australian Survey of Directors : Identification of Trends and Practices in Australian owned companies in relation to their Sales Management and Sales Forces productivity, practices and performances.

Specifications of Survey :
Profile A : Establishing performance and management standards of sales teams within Australia.

Profile B : Establishing performance and management standards of companies growth when appointing sales personnel for the first time.

Profile C : Sales Teams under the management of both profile A & B within Australia.

Criteria :

Profile A : Managing Directors
Currently employing sales people in either internal / external roles
Contributors : 1000 companies
Company Turnover : $10 million to $30 million
Operating Time : Minimum 10 years

Profile B : Managing Directors
Employed sales people within 18 months for the first time in company growth
Contributors : 300 companies
Company Turnover : $2 million to $10 million
Operating Time : Minimum 3 years

Profile C : Sales managers and sales teams From Profile A & B contributors: 150 companies

Business Categories: Manufacturing, Wholesalers, Distribution, Overseas Products Representatives, Information Technology, Telecommunications

How to contact Adele Crane and Sales Focus International

www.salesfocusintl.com

Australia 61-2-9959-2345

New Zealand 64-9-358-7323

USA 1-312-840-8559

United Kingdom 44-207-544-8565

www.ingramcontent.com/pod-product-compliance
Lightning Source LLC
Chambersburg PA
CBHW060842170526
45158CB00001B/212